Just

A

Teacher

HOW ONE PERSON
<u>CAN</u>
MAKE A DIFFERENCE

*you + your book
have changed my
life*

James O'Leary

Just a Teacher is written by Dr. James O'Hern
Copyright 2005, Dr. James O'Hern

Published and Printed by:
 Lifevest Publishing
 4901 E. Dry Creek Rd., #170
 Centennial, CO 80122
 www.lifevestpublishing.com

Printed in the United States of America

I.S.B.N. 1-59879-082-X

Just
A
Teacher

**HOW ONE PERSON
CAN
MAKE A DIFFERENCE**

By Dr. James O'Hern

Table of Contents

CHAPTER FOUR

When we were a couple of kids

1. New DCHS #8
2. Old Route 66 Still Alive and Well
3. Changing Role of Principal
4. How Racist are Our Schools?
5. Can You Play a Trumpet By Ear?
6. Freddie and His Rhythm Kings
7. My 50th Class Reunion
8. The Changing Role of the Superintendent
9. Senior Citizens Play Big Role
10. National Teaching Academy
11. The Draft is Needed for Everyone
12. Proof in the Pudding
    Class picture and caption
    Sherill's letter
    Patsy's letter
    Barb's letter
13. My Mother
14. Who is Dr. O'Hern

School days

School days

Good old golden rule days

SECTION ONE

THOSE EARLY YEARS

Billy Lee (age six) - "Why do you like school, Jimmy?"

Jimmy (age 8, curls) - "You get to drink milk and have recess."

Billy Lee - "I don't like milk."

WORDS I REMEMBER

WHEN MY MOTHER SAID
    hang up your clothes
    eat slower and chew your food
    we can't afford that
    you already have one
    respect your elders
    never hit a woman

I REMEMBER HER WORDS

WHEN MY DAD SAID

**you can have a car when you can afford it
I wish I could spend more time with you
do you think I am made of money?????
Come right home after the game**

I WISH MY DAD HAD MORE WORDS
FOR ME TO REMEMBER

Think about this one

A car company can move its factories to Mexico and claim it's a free market.

A toy company can outsource to a Chinese sub-contractor and claim it's a free market.

A major bank can incorporate in Bermuda to avoid taxes and claim it's a free market.

We can buy HP printers made in Mexico. We can buy shirts made in Bangladesh.

We can purchase almost anything we want from 20 different companies.

BUT ... heaven help the elderly who dare to buy their prescription drugs from a Canadian pharmacy. That is called un-American. And you think the pharmaceutical companies don't have a powerful lobby? THINK AGAIN.

STUDENT PICTURES THROUGHOUT BOOK

Throughout the book you will find some drawings by students. The students were in Miss Williams' fifth grade class at Saddle Ranch. They were asked to draw a picture of what they think of when they hear Dr. O'Hern's name. These students participated in a unit written by Dr. "O" on using the Road Atlas. It was called, "See the U.S.A. In Your Chevrolet." They learned how to read and use a Road Atlas. Then they had to select places in the United States they would like to visit. They used the encyclopedias and the computer to find their information. Then they wrote a 250 word summary of what they learned.

JUST A TEACHER.........INTRODUCTION
ONE PERSON CAN MAKE A DIFFERENCE

Every teacher I know has at one time said. "Why didn't I write down all those things that happen every day in my classrooms... things children say, parents comments, tales from the teacher's lounge, and those personal little chats with my principals and other administrators."

Well, much of this book is filled with those things that I HAVE written down, and I know as you read these short essays, they will bring back memories you thought you had forgotten.

This book is a series of essays written by me, Dr. James O'Hern. During my 48 years in education I have been a classroom teacher, a school principal, a member of a school board in Illinois and a consultant for the State of Illinois in gifted education and geography. I presently serve as a member of the Senior Volunteer program in this county, working in two of our finest schools. Eagle Ridge and Saddle Ranch Elementary.

The book is in part a history of the schools in Douglas County and the people who have served it so well over the years. It is in part a series of essays that I have written in various newspapers over the years. It is also a series of essays about education in general and how I have seen it over a period of 48 years. Although I am a strong sup-porter of public education, I have been very critical of many of the practices that I have been a part of. These become very obvious in the content you will read.

I have selected the title "Just a Teacher" because that is how my children answered people when they were asked "What does your Father do?" The answer was always the same. "Oh. He's JUST A TEACHER." Although I have served in the various activities listed above, I am always the most proud to say, "Yes, I AM JUST A TEACHER."

Since my arrival in Douglas County in 1987, I have been fortunate to have served this school district in many ways. I was a member of the Long Range Planning Committee for seven years. I worked on several committees that developed the standards for this district. As a Senior Volunteer I have worked in three schools where I have written and taught units on Geography, Douglas County History, Career Education and Language skills. For five years, I worked with the Discovery Program for the gifted and talented students.

My association with the Douglas County School District has convinced me that it is the finest in Colorado and probably one of the best in our nation. Not only has the district constantly ranked the highest in test scores, but it offers programs to meet the needs of all of the students. Our Alternative Education school is tops in the state. Douglas County has more charter schools than any district in Colorado that give parents choices about their child's education. There is an evening program for high school students who wish to work and still obtain their schooling. Teachers benefit from an " incentive pay plan" that has attracted visitors from all over the world.

The real feather in this district's cap is that all of these things have been accomplished in the fastest growing county in America. Each year, over 2000 new students enter a Douglas county school. For the past twenty years, at least two new schools have been built and opened each year.

A LOOK AT THE SCHOOL DISTRICT
AND DOUGLAS COUNTY

Douglas County schools are great because of many factors. It has excellent teachers, superb administrators and great facilities. But these do not exist in a vacuum. Let's take a look at some facts about the population of Douglas County that have a huge impact on our successes:

1. Douglas County population…251,900 (2003)
2. 60 percent of population is between ages 25 and 64.
3. 15 percent of population is under 15 years of age.
4. Median household income $85,000
5. 80 percent of population has college or advanced degrees
6. Castle Rock population   30,000
   Parker population 34,000
   Highlands Ranch population   80,000
                    (projected 90,000 by 2006).

I include this data because I believe that the quality of education that children receive is directly correlated to the economic income and culture of the parents. I began my administrative career in Rock Island, Illinois in a small school where we gave many of the children showers and fresh new clothes each morning to wear while in class. At the end of the day, we put their old clothes back on because if we didn't the parents would sell them. The second school in which I became the principal had a student turn-over ratio of 89 percent. I spent more time in court than I did in my office. In both of these schools, it would not have been possible to survive the CSAP program we have here in Colorado.

Somehow our politicians (and some educators) can't seem to understand the relationship between income, culture, and low test scores. The Denver Public School district is famous for condemning a school, changing the principal, and bringing in new teachers to work with the same children and the same families. I have a great essay later on in the book that deals with a legislator who says that test scores can be improved by having the parents read to their children. (You won't want to miss this one.)

When Colorado began its CSAP (Colorado Student Assessment Program, or "C-Crap" as I prefer to call it), its purpose was laudable in that it wanted to measure the achievement in Colorado. It had the support of then Governor Roy Roemer, and that support was strengthened when Bill Owens became our Governor. He latched on to "King George's" Leave No Child Behind. I prefer the term "No Child's Behind Will be Left."

CSAP soon became a vehicle for condemning schools for poor performance. (Mostly in the larger inner-cities in Colorado.) The results of this program were clear. Children in the lower economic parts of this state could not read, could not write, and could not count. Ironically, the teachers and administrators knew this years before the politicians finally "discovered it."

We will never see a school in Douglas County condemned and punished for its low scores. The factors I listed earlier will keep this from ever happening. What we do see, however, is that the low scores we see in some of our schools is directly related to the economic and culture of those school areas.

In the vast majority of Douglas County schools there is a wide range of economic factors that influence those school's test scores. In most of our schools, the test scores are just a few points from the top. It seems ludicrous to have teachers work their heads off to get their school from a 98 to 99 percentile. That is about two correct answers on a given test.

I will deal with C-CRAP later on in this book so that you can learn "HOW I REALLY FEEL".

The TV commercial says that one person cannot make a difference, so you need to join AARP - American Association of Retired People (I prefer American Association of Rich People). But I believe that as you read this book and when you complete it, you can learn that ONE PERSON CAN MAKE A DIFFERENCE. I have made a big difference in the lives of the children and teachers that I served, and you will see how one person has from time to time made a difference in my life. As "Just a Teacher" you will see just how much you have already made a difference in the lives of those children you face each day.

I hope that when you finish this book you will be as proud and happy to be JUST A TEACHER as I am.

THE SETTLERS WANTED SCHOOLS
AND THEY GOT THEM

The area known as Douglas County was a sleeping giant, until the spring of 1858 when William Levy and Oliver Russel stopped near a small creek just south of what is Franktown today. While there, they panned for gold and found a small amount. But the word went out that Gold was discovered in Douglas County, and this was the impetus for the "Pikes Peak Gold Rush.".

Although very little gold was discovered in Douglas County, the new settlers found more riches than they imagined. Here was a land of timber, water, good soil, grazing land, cool outcrops, and an ideal climate. The Russell brothers founded a small town of 500 in the area, and it was a thriving community for several years. Hundreds of artifacts have been found on this property. Many were left by the militia of Colonel Chivington as they camped here on their way to the Sand Creek Massacre. Soldiers from both the Northern and Southern armies during the Civil War camped here when they came to buy beef for the army.

Many who came for gold did not find it, but they remained in the area to become ranchers, farmers, business men, and miners. All wanted schools for their children, and that need was soon filled.

THE FONDER SCHOOL......1860'S.

Education began in the kitchen of Miriam Fonder. She set up classes for a few of the children in the neighborhood. But those classes grew so rapidly that her husband, Hubert, built her a new log cabin facility along Bijou

Gulch between Parker and Franktown. In her book, Fading Past, Susan Appleby tells of the day a group of Indians came into the school and created quite a scene. But the children were so scared that they just went right on reading aloud from their books.

Miriam was a much educated woman, but she had been badly burned and scarred as a child. Her face was covered with those scars. Her husband was later killed when he was kicked by a horse he was shoeing.

Mrs. Fonder could never have imagined what was about to happen in this area. In 1865, Sedalia became the first school district. This was even before Colorado became a state in 1876. By 1865, there were three districts with 70 students. By 1890, there were 23 schools and eleven more were added by 1900.

MORE THAN JUST A SCHOOL HOUSE

The early schools in Douglas County were the traditional one-room variety. In the room were desks, chairs, a chalk board, a pot-bellied stove, a cloak room for hanging clothes, and in the corner was a dunce stool.

The curriculum was very basic, the McGuffey reader was used, and much of it contained passages from the Bible. Spelling was very important, and class spelling bees were used. Later the district began to have spelling bees, with competition between schools.

Learning was done by lecturing and memorizing, and manners were expected at all times. Corporal punishment was applied by a hickory stick and supported by the parents.

The old tune, "School days" describes it very well.

" School days, School days
 Good old golden Rule Days,
 Reading' ritin' and 'rithmetic
 Taught to the tune of a hickory stick"

When the teacher said that 4 x 4 was 16, YOU BELIEVED HER. You did not spend a week with milk bottle caps to prove it.

In the winter months, it was the duty of the teacher to get the fire going in the morning and to put it out at night. The floor was swept daily and scrubbed once a week.

Children either walked to school, or if they were old enough, they rode their horses. If your great-grandpa tells you he walked five miles to school each day, BELIEVE HIM. I never rode a school bus to school, including walking three miles to high school each day.

Most of the children dropped out after eighth grade. Very few completed high school, and only the rich, white folks went on to college.

DOUGLAS COUNTY SCHOOL DISTRICTS BY NUMBER..1899

SCHOOL/ DISTRICT NUMBER
SEDALIA -1
ACEQUIA-16
WESTCREEK.PEMBERTON-27
FRANKTOWN- 2
LONE TREE -17
HAPPY CANYON-28
SPRING VALLEY-3
ALLISON -18
PLAINFIELD- 29
KELLY'S/GANN- 4

ROXBOROUGH-19
HILLTOP-30
BEAR CANYON- 5
CHERRY/PRATTS-20
ROUND TOP- 31
GLEN GROVE- 6
HORSE CREEK- 21
OAKLANDS- 32
INDIAN PARK-7
E. CHERRY CREEK-22
CEDAR GROVE-33
FONDER- 8
GREENLAND- 23
DEWEY- 34
DRY CREEK-/WELTE-9
ROCK RIDGE- 24
FLINTWOOD-35
CASTLE ROCK- 11
GLADE- 25
LOUVIERS- 36
LOWER LAKE GULCH-12
RATTLESNAKE-25
PARKER-36
UPPER LAKE GULCH- 13
COLUMBINE-26
BALDRIDGE-39
GOLDALE- 14
SUGAR CREEK-26
CHERRY VALLEY-40
LARKSPUR- 15
PINE GROVE-27

Each school was governed by a three person school
board, and each with its own budget. Some schools had as
many as 70 students, but that was the exception. The
school year varied, according to when the children were
needed at home to work the fields.

Several stories about these early schools can be found
in Susan Appleby's wonderful history of Douglas

County- *FADING PAST THE STORY OF DOUGLAS COUNTY.* HERE IS JUST ONE.

In December of 1913, a blizzard in Douglas County dropped more than six to ten feet of snow. By the end of the day, the snow had blocked the door, and the children could not get out. So, they spent the next three days, waiting for that snow to melt. Remember, the out-house was out back.

EDUCATION FINALLY COMES TO THE CITY

The early schools in Douglas County were one-room structures located in rural areas. However, in 1914, students from rural districts came into Parker to the new Parker school. The school was located on Main Street across from the Ruth Memorial Chapel. It was a very impressive brick structure and served the town until 1958, when the school district was consolidated into one.

The town of Castle Rock constructed a new high school, but it was immediately destroyed by a fire in 1896. The Wilcox School/Town Hall replaced it, and today that building houses the offices of the school district.

In 1897, a Cantril School was built atop "Schoolhouse Hill." It served children in the elementary grades for many years. In 1984, it was placed on the register of Historic Places.

Here are some of the early graduates from Douglas County High School .

1899....DONALD CARVER, ALDENA THOMPSON
1904..DANIEL BALL , HARRY CURTIS, GUY SMITH

1908..LENA AULSEBROOK, EDNA BENNET,
NELLIE GROSS, GEORGIA POND,
FRANCES WILLIAMS, ETHEL JONES,
MARGARET QUIEN, PERRY WILLIAMS,
ARCHIE CURTIS, LULU JONES,
CHARLES STEWART

By 1965, THE GRADUATING CLASS GREW TO 75.
LAST YEAR, OVER 200 STUDENTS GRADUATED
FROM DCHS. A COMPLETE LISTING OF GRADU-
ATES FROM 1899 TO 1964 CAN BE FOUND IN THE
HISTORY SECTION OF THE NEW LIBRARY IN
CASTLE ROCK.

Franktown School, built 1924.
DPLD, Local History Collection, #645.01

THE BILL AND DENNY SHOW

In the children's book, Danny and the Donut Machine, the donut mach malfunctioned and donuts just kept rolling out of the machine. They just kept "comin' and comin' and comin'".

This analogy fit's the scenario that in 1978 the President of Mission Viejo, Philip Reilly, announced that he was going to develop the yucca covered grassland now called Highlands Ranch. After much discussion and a lot of concern, Highlands Ranch received the blessing of the Douglas County Planning Commission and the Douglas County Commissioners. The land was purchased for 28 million dollars.

The developer announced that by 2005, 90,000 people would be living in this community. In 1981, Philip and Kay Scott purchased the first home, and they were awarded a 650 pound steer. At that time that animal would have plenty of grass to eat every day. The flood gate was opened for rampant growth, and by 1991 there were 62,000 living in these "ticky tacks" that dotted the landscape.

Where in the world was the school district going to house this influx of children? This was the issue that faced the administration and the Board of Education. The estimate was that in a very short time, over 2000 new students would be enrolling in this district each year.

In 1982, the first school was constructed and opened in Highlands Ranch. It was a joint venture, whereby the developer built the school and the district rented it for $1.00 a year. It was called North Ridge.

The district immediately addressed this problem by forming the Long Range Planning Committee. It was the task of this group to determine how much growth there would be and where these schools would be needed. Assistant

Superintendent Bill Reimer was given the assignment of overseeing this committee. It would be made up of citizens and staff members from all segments of the county.

A call went out to hire a person with experience in planning. Chosen to do this was Denny Hill. He was to remain in this position for eight years. Denny now works with Strategic Resources West in Castle Rock.

At first, many people questioned the projection of 90,000 by 2005. Why would that many people come to this area. There was no commercial development in Douglas County, and the land was covered with desert vegetation. But the district could not afford to reject or ignore this number. These items had to be addressed:

1. Where will the people choose to build and live?
2. How can the district afford to build these schools
    and staff them?
3. How can boundary changes be kept to a minimum?
4. How can the district rely on bond elections to get
    the money?

These questions became the agenda for every meeting of the LRPC. Denny Hill was handed the crystal ball and told to "go to it".

At meeting after meeting, Denny presented the population projections for the next five years. A big part of our challenge was that the developer had to set aside land for a school in each area. In many towns, that land has to be purchased, and often at inflated prices.

During the seven years that I served on this committee I was constantly amazed at how accurate Denny's numbers were. All in all, about 98 percent.

Because each time a new school was built, boundaries had to be changed, and this was not popular with the parents. But month after month members of the planning committee went to community meetings to explain the changes needed.

Money had to also be obtained from bond elections. Again, the LRPC members became the sales-people for this project. All of these bond elections passed except one in ___1992___ . And that one passed the following year when parents realized the consequences of not passing it - class size, longer days, etc.

Perhaps the most important change in district policy was putting all new schools on a year-round calendar. That meant children and teachers would attend school for nine weeks and then be off for three.

The district learned from the problems that happened in Jefferson County that families with more than one child must be on the same track. This plan allowed for three schools to house the traditional four schools. It saved the district millions of dollars over the years.

While it was hoped that the secondary schools could also be on year-round, it was not possible because of the extra curricular activities.

The development of Highlands Ranch immediately created new development in the entire county. The populations of Castle Rock and Parker exploded. In 1986, Castle Rock had a population of 3000. Today it exceeds 30,000. Parker grew from 2500 in 1986 to over 40,000 today.

Not only did the larger towns grow, but people rushed into areas like Founders Village, Roxborough, Sedalia, Kiowa, Franktown, Castle Pines and others, and schools were needed in each area.

Tax relief came in the expansion of commercial businesses. Parker and Castle Rock had mini-malls and the largest factory outlet stores in the country. Parker too had a mini-mall and a new hospital. All of these have brought new tax dollars to the county, and in Colorado that means tax relief for a homeowner.

Many of the elementary schools that have been on the year-round calendar for many years are now returning to the traditional calendar. That is because these neighborhoods have matured and there is no growth in them.

But in spite of that, we now have over 50 schools in Douglas County and more are on the drawing board.

What is really ironic is that it is about the same number of schools we had back in the early 1900's when the district was consolidated.

Both Denny and Bill Reimer are no longer with the district. Bill is basking in the beautiful town of Crested Butte and Denny is working in the planning field. They maybe gone, but what they left behind will never be replaced and we owe them our deep gratitude for what they have done.

THE COLORADO DEPARTMENT OF EDUCATION SAYS "WELCOME"

In 1985, I took early retirement and spent the next two years as the editor of a local history magazine. Then in 1987, I ran for the Board of Education and was elected by the largest vote in the history of our county. That was not because were such wonderful people, but rather we promised to fire the superintendent if we were elected, and we did at the first meeting. I also did some substitute teaching for $30.00 per day.

So when I moved to Colorado, subbing became an option. This was my introduction to the Colorado Department of Education. But, to do any subbing, I had to be certified by this state. I was granted a provisional certificate to use while waiting for the final one.

The next step was to obtain some more paper work from the State of Illinois and all of the colleges I had attended. After that six week period, I received the following information from the Colorado Department of Education:

1. YOU ARE NOT QUALIFIED TO TEACH AT THE ELEMENTARY LEVEL.

I had been certified in Illinois for 25 years to teach at the elementary level. In addition, I had been an elementary teacher and school principal and held an elementary administrative certificate. But, —————

2. YOU ARE ONLY QUALIFIED TO TEACH MATH AT THE HIGH SCHOOL LEVEL.

I had never taught at a high school, and had no course work in math.

3. YOU WILL NEED TO TAKE 24 ADDITIONAL HOURS OF COURSE WORK TO BE CERTIFIED IN COLORADO.

I already had a Bachelor of Science Degree in Elementary Administration, a Masters Degree in Secondary Education and a PhD in Alternative Education.

I RESPONDED TO THIS LETTER BY STATING "I WILL NEVER TEACH IN COLORADO."

While waiting for that letter from CDE, I went and placed my name on the DC sub list. I received a call one day to teach at the new Highlands Ranch High School. It was for a 7th grade math class.

Like most substitutes, I knew I was going to be challenged by someone in that room. This is what all "subs" have to endure. So one boy decided to make his move, and when he did I told him to move himself to the back of the room until he could get his act together.

After class, the assistant principal came to my room, and she told me that in Douglas County we don't punish children. She said that I would have to apologize to the student and his parents. I did so, and that was the first and last day I have ever subbed in this district.

The irony is that for fifteen years now I have gone into dozens of ELEMENTARY classrooms as part of the volunteer program for seniors.

I am sure that many of you who just read this story can relate to it.

GETTING ACQUAINTED...GETTING INVOLVED

When we moved to Colorado in 1987, we decided to purchase a home in Acres Green. This is a subdivision located on the northern boundary of Douglas County. At that time, we didn't know anything about the county. All we knew was that my wife could see the peak on Mt. Evans from the kitchen window, and we had the cash to pay full price. We didn't even know there were three rooms in the basement.

Although I was legally retired (my membership in AARP validated that fact), I knew I somehow wanted to remain involved in education in some way. I had four options:

1. Get certified and do some substitute teaching. Pay
    was very good in Colorado.
2. Volunteer in the classroom in the nearby
    elementary school.
3. Serve on district committees.
4. Write education columns in local newspapers.

In the end, three of the four opened up for me. Only substitute teaching became a disaster for me. (A later essay will tell about this catastrophe.)

The first step I took was to meet the local administrators of Douglas County Schools. This meeting took place in a series of very small offices in an upstairs building on Wilcox Street. It was there that I met the new " Sup", Dr. Rick O'Connell and his three assistants.

The Douglas County School District was quite small, especially compared to the district back in Illinois. The enrollment was about the same, and the size of the county was geographically equal, but it differed in this way. My county in Illinois was made up of six separate school districts, each with its own school board, superintendent, bus service, and each had a football stadium. Douglas County had one of each, including a single stadium in Castle Rock. But that was explained to me that even though we had three high schools in the county, the band program was far more important than the sports teams.

At that time the district consisted of a high school in Parker, Castle Rock and Highlands Ranch, middle schools in those areas, and elementary schools in Cherry Valley, Highlands Ranch, Larkspur, Franktown, Sedalia, Castle Rock, and Parker.

About a week later I read in the paper that the district was beginning a new program called "The Senior Tax Exchange." So I contacted a man named Lowell Baumunk. He had been the first superintendent of the district when it was re-organized in 1958. He was now retired but remained to oversee this new program. A complete essay will be found later in this book about this program and how it has grown over the years. But the general idea was to obtain senior citizens to work in the district, and they would be paid for their service. That money could be used to supplement the property taxes of the citizens.

A few years later, the program had to be renamed because of tax laws, and then we had the Senior Volunteer Program. I enrolled in this program and began my volunteer work at Acres Green Elementary, just two blocks from our home.

In 1989, I read in the local paper that the editor wanted

citizens to write columns in the Daily News Press. It was at this time that I met Richard Bangs, the Editor of this paper. I wrote education columns each week for the next 12 years. This was an experience I truly enjoyed.

About this time I also read that the school district wanted citizens to serve on the Long Range Planning Committee. I served on this committee for seven years, and it was here that I began a life-long friendship with Bill Reimer, "Assistant Superintendent in Charge of Everything That Moved," and Denny Hill, his guru assistant. Their story will be told in a later essay.

So far, four of my goals had been met, and it became clear that my retirement days were not going to be spent in a rocking chair.

It was now obvious that I was going to be involved in the profession that I love so much. This was very important to me because I had seen so many friends retire, and they just faded into nothing. My own step-father worked for Walgreens for forty years, and three years after he retired he was dead. At least, it seemed that I would not suffer the same fate that he did.

THE MAN WHO COULD NEVER BE REPLACED ... DR. PAT GRIPPE

When Dr. Rick O'Connell heard of the purchase and development of Highlands Ranch and the projection of 90,000 people by 2005, I doubt he had any idea of what that would mean to his school district.

Rick was a highly respected superintendent. He knew the names and faces of all of his teachers, and visited them regularly in their classrooms. But that was all about to change.

Early in his career, Rick learned the value of having very competent people to get the job done. He had to find ways to deal with this massive influx of people, and he had to have people who could see that the quality of education remained as high as it had been for years.

In 1985, he brought in Mrs. Ellen Bartlett to head the personnel department. Imagine 2000 new kids a year and the number of teachers and administrators needed to handle that explosion. Ellen came to Douglas County from Fort Collins and was recommended by an employee of the district.

In 1985, Bill Reimer became the Assistant Superintendent in Charge of Anything That Moves. Joining him in 1988 was Denny Hill, an expert in planning. It was his job to tell us where the people will be and where the new schools will be placed.

But his real prize "hire" was Dr. Pat Grippe. Pat came from the Aurora district and was to become the interim principal at the new Ponderosa High School in Parker. Two years later he was appointed the Assistant Superintendent in Charge of Curriculum. Although he was technically the

"Assistant Superintendent in Charge of Curriculum" he was really more than that. Many of the people in our district today do not realize that so many programs we have today all started at the desk of "Dr. Pat". Let me just share two.

Building Resource Teacher (BRT)

In all of our schools today, we have a person called a "BRT" (Building Resource Teacher). Pat knew that with the number of new students and teachers coming to the district, someone should be there to make the transition as smooth as possible. That person should be there to assist new teachers and to support the new staffs that will be formed. This person should be a "master teacher" with the skills and knowledge to do these things.

No sooner did the words "BRT" come out of the mouth of Dr. Grippe than there was bitter opposition. Teachers did not feel the need for such a position, and that money could be used to increase the pay for teachers. The administrators were not open to the idea either. This had always been their job to help new teachers, and the money could be used in better ways.

It was at this time that I was writing a weekly education column in the Castle Rock Daily News Press. I too, thought this was a crazy idea, and I wrote several columns in opposition to it.

But Pat was determined to implement this new program, and so several teachers were hired to be the BRTs. The survival of this program depended on the new teachers that were placed in these schools. Some did very well; others did not.

Today, the BRT program is generally well accepted throughout the district.

D.C. Oaks Academy

Although we had a district with very high test scores, we did have a small populous of kids who just couldn't make it in the regular secondary schools. The drop out rate was rising as was the increase in truancy.

Dr. Grippe knew there was a need for an alternative education program for those kids. A complete essay is devoted to alternative education in this book.

One of Pat's greatest concerns was that the parents in Douglas County have choices in the kind of education their child could receive. He was instrumental in establishing charter schools, the Discovery Program for gifted children, the International Baccalaureate Program for high schoolers. The Advanced Placement classes and the Eagle Academy have been highly successful. All of these programs are described in enclosed essays.

One of my most interesting assignments in the district was surveying Douglas County High School graduates to learn what and how they were doing in their lives today. Dr. Grippe asked me to do this survey, and we ended up with a very interesting report in booklet form. It was a real eye-opener. I have not seen a copy of this book for many years, but I imagine it is around somewhere.

WHERE DID THESE NAMES COME FROM?

In my early years in education, I was associated with schools that had very traditional names. I attended the Webster Elementary School in Quincy, Illinois. I graduated from Burlington High School in Burlington, Iowa. My first teaching job was in Eugene Field Elementary in Rock Island, Illinois, and my first principal's assignment was in Lincoln Elementary in that city. When I moved to Galesburg, Illinois, I became the principal of Steele Middle School. Mr. Steele was one of the early superintendents in that town.

The practice in most school districts was to name the schools after presidents, heroes and local dignitaries. In America, almost every state has a Washington, Lincoln, Jefferson and Adams Elementary school. Most of the high schools were named after the town in which they were located.

Special events brought on the naming of schools after John F. Kennedy, Martin Luther King Jr. and the tragic accident of the Challenger in 1986. Aboard was Christine McAuliffe, the first teacher in space.

However, when I moved to Douglas County the names of schools just blew my mind. The schools that were here had been named after early schools like Franktown, Sedalia, and Larkspur. Franktown was the name of the town founded by Frank Gardner. Sedalia was named for the Missouri hometown of its founder. Larkspur was the yellow flower that grew along the railroad tracks. Then there was Castle Rock Elementary, South Street Elementary, Ponderosa High School and Highlands Ranch High School.

Then something happened. Some people wanted to name new schools in the traditional way. Others wanted to honor such local historical people like William Cantril. However, for some reason, the School Board voted to not allow any new school to be named after a person or a subdivision.

The result of that board action was that all future schools be named by a committee of parents in each new school. So after sixteen years of adding new schools, we ended up with school names in four categories...historical people, geographic features, animals, and cultural terms of the West.

Here is a list of some of the schools we have here in Douglas County:

I. CARRY OVER FROM EARLY SCHOOLS

Douglas County High School, Ponderosa High School, Castle Rock Middle School, Castle Rock Elementary, Franktown, Sedalia, and Larkspur Elementary. We also had the D.C. Oakes Alternative High School.

II. SCHOOLS NAMED FOR GEOGRAPHIC FEATURES

Mountain Ridge Middle School, Rocky Heights H.S., Mountain Vista H.S., Thunderridge H.S., Sand Creek, Timber Trail, Platte River Charter, Coyote Creek, Legacy Point, Pine Grove, Summit Grove, Wildcat Mountain, Plum Creek, Acres Green and Fox Creek Elementary.

III. ANIMALS AND WESTERN CULTURE

Chaparral H.S., Bear Canyon , Eagle Ridge, Iron Horse,

Saddle Ranch, Soaring Hawk, Trailblazer, Wildcat Mountain, Eagle Academy.

When a new school is about to open, a committee of parents and students is formed to select a name for that school. I have never been to one of these meetings, but it must be an experience to hear some of the suggestions.

When the new school in Lone Tree was completed, the name "Eagle Ridge" was selected, I can't imagine when the last eagle was spotted on that site. One has to also question how the name "Lone Tree" was selected for that community.

The name "Iron Horse" in Parker was selected because the early railroad from Denver to Colorado Springs ran across the site on which the school was built. A portion of the railroad track lies in front of the school.

When the early pioneers came West, they traveled on several trails. One was Cherokee Trail, and it came across the prairie into Russellville and North to Parker. That school is located on that trail.

D.C. Oakes started the gold rush to Colorado by sending word back East of the huge gold strike at Russellville. The word went out, "PIKES PEAK OR BUST." I still can't figure out why he was chosen for the name of the Alternative High School.

Many of the animals selected roamed this land in Douglas County before they were replaced by the building boom. I can recall that when I moved here 20 years ago, a large herd of deer frequented the area behind the Post Office on Quebec for their morning drink of water. Today, four schools occupy that land.

I also recall the time that Highlands Ranch had a heavy

rainfall, and several of the tiny creeks overflowed their banks. Along with the water came several hundred rattlesnakes. I am sure the developer would deny this story, but the early residents won't.

Since the county is still growing and new schools are being added each year, it will be interesting to see what new names will be chosen. So let's look at what is left...

Skunks, snakes, prairie dogs, wolves, swamps, and bunkhouse. Spurs, ram-rod, barbed wire, and snuff. But somehow, "Skunk Valley Elementary" just doesn't do it for me. But neither does "Legacy Point."

MASON DIXON LINE IS SLOWLY BEING DRAWN IN THE COUNTY

We all know that Douglas County is the fastest growing county in the country. It is also one of the richest in the nation. Our school district is one of the finest in Colorado, and in general the quality of life is quite good. But on the other side of the coin is the fact that we are very rapidly becoming the most "snobbish county" in Colorado.

It is very clear that a "Mason-Dixon Line" has been drawn between Castle Rock and Northern Douglas County. As a result, the power and money now lie just North of that line. There are enough people in Highlands Ranch and Lone Tree to control every election. Although that vote has been positive in the past, we may begin to see a change in upcoming school bond elections.

For many years, Douglas County was a very prosperous rural area. We are the second largest "horse county" in America. Our history is one of agriculture, ranching and mining. Now the only mining we do is to deposit our fat pay checks each month.

There is no doubt that we are now the best school district in Colorado. It is important for each school to want to be the best, but not at the price of isolating itself from other schools. Ask any teacher when was the last time they visited another school in the district to see how other practices are working. About the only time principals exchange ideas is at the many meetings held at the main office.

More and more schools are having some parents saying. "We won't go to THAT school", and they are allowed to attend any school of their choice. I know of one school that has a classroom of only nineteen children because five parents who live at that school district in a home with a four car garage refused to attend THAT school. That is snobbery.

The only high school that can really be called "multi-cultural" is Douglas County High School. Kids from both sides of the Line attend that school. The students there realize that a student who is wearing boots instead of $100 NIKE shoes is not culturally deprived. It is the only school where students realize that "stuff" on those boots is not mud, and the smell of pigs is MONEY, not disgusting.

One of the real vestiges of the past is our annual county fair. I was at the parade and watched the many people who participated. I was really upset that although we now have five high schools in this county, only one of our high school bands participated in that parade. That was the DCHS band, and they were outstanding. There were units from as far away as Boulder, but only one local band participated in the parade. One band parent from another high school told me that their director doesn't like to march in parades .

There were children from cheerleading classes, gymnastics groups, and several 4H units. But all from South of the Mason Dixon Line. I was amazed to learn that we have over 30 4H clubs in Douglas County. There was even a Hispanic marching unit. But you could count the people who live North of the Line who witnessed this parade.

I will admit I am a little old fashioned. I believe in community, whether it be the county or our own neighborhoods. Many people here still do not know the names of the people in their neighborhoods. We have become a series of bedroom communities, where we drive to work and then come home, awaiting the next day's drive. Many people know the names of their ski lift operator better than they do the people who live around them.

The only real community we have left seems to be our local schools. We still see people there working together for a common cause. I am sure we will never see that expanded beyond the walls of the classroom.

Those who live in Acres Green have seen how one community can encircle another, with little regard for the outcome of that growth. When I moved into our home twelve years ago, I could see Mt. Evans from our back porch. Now I can see the new Holiday Inn Motel, Mt. Pep Boys, Mt. Sams, Mt. Country Buffet and a multitude of restaurants. That is the price we are all paying for this growth. Developers call it progress. Others call it greed.

It is somewhat comforting that many of our towns are having events of their own that bring people together. In Highlands Ranch we can see the Scottish Festival and Parker has several local events. Many neighborhoods are even having concerts in the park.

So for now, we old fogies will have to admit that those days of going to County Fair and watching county parades are over. There is no thought of moving because Douglas County is still the greatest place to live, and we will just ignore the snobs.

GET YOUR HAIR DONE BEFORE YOU
GET EVALUATED

When I became a principal in 1962, the job I hated most was evaluating teacher performance. The process was for me to take a list of criteria into the classroom, sit in the back and watch acts I and II by the teacher. I was also told to let the principal inform the teacher on which day and what time this ceremony would take place. That gave the teacher time to shower, shave, get her hair done and dress as suggestive as possible.

The principal had to use the district check list as a guide that consisted of such things as voice, mannerisms, and many other non-educational factors. Following this rite of passage act, the teacher and principal met and went over the list.

When I moved to Galesburg, Illinois and became the principal of a new middle school, I decided to try a new approach to evaluating. At the beginning of the year, I asked each teacher to list three professional and three personal goals that he or she wanted to reach this year. These might include 1. Get more involved in school activities or 2. Make my lesson plans more easy to implement in the classroom. Many of my teachers were quite uneasy with this method at first, but most really enjoyed that final conference. Teachers get better under this system because they want to do so, not because they did better on that one day they got to perform and get their hair done.

D.C. PERFORMANCE PAY PLAN GAINS NATIONAL ATTENTION

Several " merit pay" plans have been tried throughout this country, but eventually most fail for a variety of reasons.

1. It uses administrators to judge performance.
2. There is usually favoritism and it is inevitable.
3. It ends costing too much to pay for performance.
4. Too often the plan is created by central administration and handed down to the people involved.

In the mid-nineties, Doug Hartman, president of the Douglas County Federation of Teachers and Mrs. Ellen Bartlett, Director of Personel for the school distruct got together to discuss the possibility of improving instruction in the district. They began to zero in on developing a performance pay plan that would not be subjected to the four items listed above. They shared a common goal of wanting to find ways to improve teacher performance.

They realized that the general public and the business community generally favored such plans. But most teachers did not because of the reasons listed before.

In this essay, I am not going to spell out in detail the performance pay plan that was finally adopted. If you are in the district, you know those , and if you are not in the district, there are several articles on "Google."

Instead, I will mention some things about that plan that are unique and have led to its tremendous success. They make good guidelines for future planning.

1. GO SLOWLY AND GET COMMUNITY INVOLVEMENT

In Douglas County a lot of different people from the school community and the business world were involved. The process started from scratch. It was not a proposal written out by either Doug or Ellen and passed to you to look over. The exchange of ideas was fierce, but sensible.

2. KEEP THE TOTAL COMMITTEE INVOLVED

Too many times the committee starts out with a lot of involvement, then slowly the number begins to dwindle. This committee remained in tact throughout the process.

3. BE SURE THE INCENTIVES TO BE USED ARE FAIR AND WORKABLE.

If money is going to be a part of the incentive to improve, be sure that the amounts are fair and workable. You cannot pay the same amount for a "Master Teacher" as you pay the man who takes tickets at a basketball game. Be very sure that the Board of Education can afford the payments.

4. THE PLAN MUST INCLUDE AN OPPORTUNITY TO ATTAIN DIFFERENT LEVELS OF ACCOMPLISHMENT.

When you read the detailed plan adopted you will see the many ways that teachers can choose their path of opportunities. They can work as a school team to improve map skills, or they can continue taking college work.

5. THE FINAL PLAN MUST HAVE WAYS FOR ON-GOING EVALUATION.

Far to many plans like this adopt the plan and then let it swim on its own. There must be constant evaluation of the content and process.

PERHAPS THE BEST PROOFS THAT THIS PLAN IS WORKING ARE FACTS:

1. It has received International recognition. Several countries around the world have come to see it in action.

2. Teacher approval is still very high.

3. It has become a real plus for recruiters of new staff.

4. Both Doug and Ellen have left the district, but the plan remains.

ANOTHER BENEFIT IS:
IN DOUGLAS COUNTY YOU CAN BECOME A GREAT TEACHER AND YOU NEVER HAVE TO TAKE A BATH OR GET YOUR HAIR DONE.

SECTION
TWO

CLASSROOM
CAPERS

Readin'

And 'ritin

And 'rithmetic

Taught to the tune
Of a hickory stick

STORIES YOU WON'T WANT TO FORGET

Every teacher I know wishes he or she could have written down some of the stories that have happened to him or her. Here are a few that I have taken time to jot down.

1. THAT MORNING SHOWER

My first principal assignment was at a small school located on an island in Rock River, in Rock Island, Illinois. The school had about 60 children, and the families were very poor "white trash" and very dirty people. When their children came to school each morning, we had about ten that we gave a shower to. We kept clean clothes on hand, and changed their dirty clothes for the day. If we gave the children clean clothes to take home, the parents would have sold them to get beer or wine money. The real irony is that at the end of the second week at this school, we had a bad flood, and the school washed away and was closed down.

2. LINCOLN WOULD HAVE TURNED OVER IN HIS GRAVE.

My second school was Lincoln Elementary in the downtown area of Rock Island. The school had been built in the 1880's, and the walls were more than 3 feet thick. The school was quite a mix. We had a few children from families that were professors at Augustana College. The rest were poor white trash where the police made daily home calls. Several calls were to those Mothers who were using their 12 year old daughters for prostitution. We also had three attempts at arson, and finally one night two girls from the junior high next door to us, set fire to their building and completely destroyed that building.

3. COOKE ELEMENTARY..A CONTRADICTION CULTURES.

I was assigned to one of the five new middle schools in Galesburg, Illinois to open in 1967. But problems arose and delayed the opening for a year. Consequently, I was assigned to work at an elementary school in the very poor section of town for a year. This school was about 90 percent Black students, and the school was in shambles.

In my kindergarten class there were two twin boys. I noticed one day that these boys were coming to school on alternate days. When I asked my secretary what was going on, she said, "Lets make a home visit."

When we arrived at this home, I noticed that it had a dirt floor. There were five children in the family, but only three rooms in the house. There was no inside bathroom.

In talking to the Mother, we learned of our problem. The boys only had ONE PAIR OF SHOES, and they wore them on alternate days. I took the boys to Sears and got them each a pair of shoes, and the attendance problem was solved.

But this is not the end of this story, all five of these children graduated from college. One evening I was playing my trumpet for a party at the mental hospital. Standing in the back of the room was this tall, very attractive Black woman. At intermission she came up and said she was Linda_____and was the supervisor of the hospital. She had a Master's Degree in Hospital Administration from the University of Illinois. She also said the twin boys were married and living in California. She also reminded me of the shoe incident.

IS EVERY CHILD REALLY GIFTED?????????

Many educators believe that every child is gifted. Certainly most parents do believe this. That may be true if gifted mean "talented", then that may be more acceptable. But every child does not have high intellectual capacity, and every classroom is made up with a higher degree of both mental capacity and talents.

Some teachers will teach to the middle, some to the very low, but few ever really teach to the very high. That is not a fault, it is simply a fact.

This is probably the best reason to have separate classes for those very bright students. Call them "gifted" or whatever you want to call them, but there is a segment of our school populations that needs that special challenge.

I first became involved in gifted education in 1958, when I taught a group of 12 very bright sixth graders in the history of our county. We met on Saturday morning and did all of our work in the field. We visited historic sites and visited with old timers who shared many interesting stories with us.

Illinois has been a leader in gifted education since the 1970's, and in 1982, the Legislature passed legislation that required funding for the teaching of the gifted child.

I was asked that year to serve as a consultant for the state gifted program. My task was to make sure that all children who were "gifted" had been identified, so that district would receive the money to set up a program for them. I focused on the small rural districts. Many of these had gifted children, but not in numbers large enough to have a "Program". While I tried to eliminate "Gifted on Tuesday" classes, it was difficult to find the time for any other approaches.

The state also established a school for the very brightest children in Illinois. These students lived on campus for three years in an abandoned high school in Aurora. It is ironic, but the first thing the students did was to do away with letter grades. I had three of my former sixth graders attend this school. One year, one of my ex-students nominated me as the teacher who made the greatest impression on him. Once again, one person can make a difference.

In Douglas County, the gifted program, Discovery, began in 2000 in two schools-Acres Green and Northridge. Children in grades 2-3, 4-5, and 5-6 met at these schools and had all of their classes with one teacher per grade.

I began working with the 2-3 class at Acres Green. The teachers had the freedom and responsibility to develop their own curriculum. While these teachers were very talented, they did not have a degree in gifted education (maybe that is why the program was so successful).

In time, I worked with all three grade levels with some very talented teachers. The classes in which I worked did units on diagramming, world history, and many math projects. Several field trips took place at all grade levels. The sixth grade class did a detailed study of Africa and the Middle Ages.

The program has grown now to several schools in the district and are housed throughout the county. After working with these classes for five years, I would like to make these suggestions.

1. Screen students and have a two year evaluation period. I find that many of these students do not belong in the gifted program.
2. Instead of arranging classes by grade level, classes should be organized by the intellectual level of the child.

3. The CSAP scores of the gifted students are counted in with the home school. They should be separated and analyzed separately. The present system is not fair to the home school or those children in the class.

4. At the present time the children can have the same teacher for as long as three years. This should be adjusted.

When working with gifted students, it is important to remember that these children do not need more of something, they need a very different approach to their learning. That is why it is so difficult to meet the needs of gifted children in a regular classroom. While the regular children may be assigned four pages of Math, the teacher is inclined to assign twice that many to the gifted child.

An even bigger problem can be the evaluation of their work. The regular classroom teacher will give a test on the Bill Of Rights, and often the questions are multiple choice, true-false or some other shortened form. The gifted child should be evaluated by using high level thinking skills. For example.

"The Bill of Rights was written to protect the citizens. Of these rights, list the five that you feel are the most important." You can see that a much higher level of thinking is needed to answer this question.

The picture on the next page is of a class of gifted students that I worked with. This was done at the time that the area where Sky Ridge Medial Center now stands was just being developed. While the story was well written, reporters often get the names of people wrong.

It should also be mentioned that providing for the gifted in the Discovery program is not the only challenging programs offered to them. The program is offered at the middle school level in certain subjects. In the high schools the students have the International Baccalaureate program, along with Advanced Placement classes. These classes allow students to enter college at a sophomore level.

I have never understood why some educators do not believe in special education for these gifted children. In fact, this school district resisted starting a gifted program for our children. The Discovery program was really an off-shoot of the first charter schools.

The biggest complaint I have for gifted education is the tremendous pressure that is put on these children by the parents. But I guess that is normal and something these kids will have to deal with all of their lives.

Acres Green Elementary students learned about urban planning including population projections, enrollment tabulations and the incorporation of real life planning principles. School volunteer Dr. Jim O'Hern designed the lesson plans for students, and Lone Tree city planner Sarah Spencer-Workman visited the students to talk to them about the city's design guidelines and the process of annexation.
Photo by Lance Dutton

TEACHING CITY KIDS ABOUT FARM LIFE IS A REAL CHALLENGE

Teaching children anything these days is a real challenge, but you ain't seen anything until you try to teach city children about life on the farm. We have a whole generation that doesn't know a horse from a pig, and when it comes to farm structures we are in a different world.

For four years, I taught a unit on Colorado and Douglas County History and Geography to fourth graders in the Discovery classes. These were students in the gifted program. These young people were all city folks, and for the most part they had never been exposed to a farm animal except the horse on a merry-go-round.

Now, before I go on condemning these youngsters, let me admit that I too am a city guy. I thought for years that we got chocolate milk from brown cows. I didn't know a silo from a solo. So, I can't chastise these children for not knowing few things about farm life.

I only began to know anything about life on a farm when I married a farm girl. I can't count the times she laughed at my ignorance. But I have learned, and I try to share what I now know with these students.

We began our study of Colorado by learning the three regions of Colorado: the Plains, the Mountains. and the Plateau. To most people who have never been to this state, they believe that all we have are the mountains. If you come to Colorado from Illinois by train, you will travel across country at night. That is so you can't see what the eastern part of our state looks like. When you return to Illinois, you also travel at night.

To really bring the message home, we spent two days looking at slides I have taken of these regions. They are astonished to see the round green corn fields of the eastern plains, and they learned why that land has to be irrigated.

I use a lot of slides in my teaching of geography. I want children to begin to think like a geographer, not necessarily become a geographer.

They are astonished to learn how the south eastern plains produce the finest cantaloupes in America, and that an onion field looks like a poppy grove, filled with red flowers. They learned what role feed lots played to a cattle rancher. As one child told me, "A pure-bred cow is one that has the same mommy and daddy."

To get my slides, I often spend two or three days in the field before I use them in the classroom. Slides must tell a story and they must raise questions. Far too many people only take a slide picture when they have Aunt Bessie pose in front of a statue of some pioneer.

On one of my trips, I came across an old, rusty thrashing machine that was slowly rusting in a field. I asked the children what they thought this machine was. After several very wild guesses, one little girl replied. "I believe that is what they use to scoop up the cow poop." To her, I could only reply, "That is the biggest pooper-scooper you will ever see."

Children are fascinated with slides, especially ones that tell a story. When children study Colorado history in fourth grade, they have few resources to use in that study. That is especially true when they try to learn about physical and cultural geography. They often miss the fact that the history of Colorado is its physical geography. Just think of the historical events that are the direct result of our geography. I tell the children that without the mountains, Colorado would be another Kansas, and we don't need two of them.

There are many slides that show the names of our towns, and we talked about how these names came to be -Cripple Creek, Tin Cup, Grand Junction, Sedalia, Aspen, Silverton and the list goes on and on. In Colorado, the town sign shows elevation. In Illinois, the sign shows population. (A very good idea for Douglas County.

The purpose of this unit was to help children learn to observe the world around them and to ask questions. WHAT IS WHERE? WHY? AND WHAT OF IT?"

Very few of them will ever become geographers. But all can travel from place to place and see something beside the Mc Donald's Golden Arches or the sign for the nearest bathroom.

WHAT IS WHERE? WHY? AND WHAT OF IT?

From the fall of 1957 to the summer of 1958, I attended Western Illinois University in Macomb, Illinois. By the end of my third year of classroom teaching I had decided to continue my education and complete the requirements for a Masters Degree in Elementary Education. An increase in salary played a small role in that decision, but I was really concerned about how many teachers could benefit from my being an elementary school administrator.

A part of that curriculum was completing a course in Social Studies. I chose geography for some reason, and it proved to be the best decision I ever made. My professors were Dr. Robert Gabler and Mr. Arlen Fentem. The course consisted of some basic geographic concepts, plus ways to teach the content in the classroom.

The class also required the writing of a paper on geography methods in the classroom. I wrote a paper on "Panty Hose Geography." It was a technique that my wife and I created, using panty hose boxes we obtained at a local department store. In the boxes we placed cards with maps and geography questions on them.

Dr. Gabler was so pleased with this paper that he gave me an "A" on it and asked me if he could publish it in the Illinois Geographic Society newsletter. One cannot describe the feeling one gets when he sees his "by-line" on a published newsletter.

But this was only the beginning. He invited me to come to Los Angeles and present my paper at the

National Geographic Society Convention (this is the big one). I was to fly to California, present my paper, and then drive back with Dr. Gabler and his family. The school district was not happy with spending the money for the plane fare, but finally they paid it.

(It was on this trip that I was introduced to a margarita. In fact I had six that night. I woke up next morning looking for the camel).

But, this was not even the ending of my story. About two weeks after I returned from California, I received a telephone call at school. It was from a Mr. Stan Christodolus, the senior editor at Silver Burdette Publishing Company. He said he wanted me to write a book for them. I thought it was a prank, so I hung up. Immediately, he called back and began to tell me what he wanted.

His company was creating a new 7th grade Social Studies Textbook. He said a Dr. Kimball was writing the geographic content, and he wanted me to write the Teacher's Edition and a workbook to accompany the text. He said that he had heard my presentation in Los Angeles and wanted my style for this new geographic concept.

The irony here was that Dr. Kimball was a retired Professor from the University of Indiana. But he was now retired and living on the island of Sicily (off coast of Italy). He was to write and type the content, and then mail it to the publisher in New Jersey for editing, and then it would be forwarded to me in Galesburg, Illinois. From that copy, I was to write the ways for the teachers to teach it. Included in this writing was a set of standards for each lesson. I had never written a standard in my life. But I had always used them long before they were re-invented.

There is even more to my Geography experience. Stan told me I had two options. I could take a $5,000 advance now, or I could be paid based on the sale of the book. These were called royalties. For some reason, I chose the royalties, and what a stroke of luck that was. So successful was the book that state adoptions were made in Texas, New York, Illinois, and California. That means every child in seventh grade in those states would be using this textbook. So, for the next ten years, I received the royalties. Before they had run out, I had collected over $50,000. This helped pay for those wonderful trips to Europe and Africa (described in culture essay).

This was a time when the U.S. Department of Education created and funded a series of Summer workshops in Geography. Teachers were selected from all over the country to come to Western Illinois University, with all expenses paid plus a sizable stipend to come and learn how to teach geography, Dr. Gabler was in charge of the workshop at Western, so he asked me to teach the "how" part of the session for a very nice salary.

One of the professors in this workshop was Arlen Fentem. He was an outstanding geographer, and he taught me and the class his definition of GEOGRAPHY.

WHAT IS WHERE? WHY? AND WHAT OF IT?

Traditionally, Geography has been teaching the '"What is Where" part of the discipline. Place location. You may well remember memorizing all the locations of states and countries.

Let's look at the city of Denver, using our definition. WHERE IS DENVER? Denver is located on the East side of the Rocky Mountains.

WHY IS DENVER THERE?

As people came West, they settled on the Eastern side of the mountains before they attempted to cross these mountains. They opened stores, banks, hotels and homes to serve the people who were coming West. The town was located at the end of many of early trails and there was plenty of water in Denver.

WHAT OF IT?

Once the growth began, more and more people came here. Denver was also the site of the new railroads. These railroads also increased the population of such places as Sedalia, Castle Rock and other communities.

In the Geography classes I teach in second, third, fourth and fifth grades. I teach the children a song, using the definition I learned...sing along with me now..

WHAT IS WHERE? WHY? WHAT OF IT?
THAT IS WHAT WE'RE GOING TO SHOUT
WHAT IS WHERE? WHY ?WHAT OF IT?
THAT'S WHAT GEOGRAPHY'S ALL ABOUT.

Two other interesting things happened as a result of that Geography class I took at Western. In 1958, my paper on Panty Hose Geography won the national award in Geography. The following year I was selected as the Outstanding Geography Teacher in Illinois. In that same year I became a consultant for the state of Illinois and taught several workshops throughout the state.

THE D.C. OAKES ACADEMY ALTERNATIVE HIGH SCHOOL IN DOUGLAS COUNTY.

In 1991, Dr. Pat Grippe learned of two boys who were having real problems in their middle school. He believed that there were probably other children in those middle schools who might be having the same type of problems. Some of these problems were drug related, but the vast majority were children who were having family situations that caused them to do poorly in school.

Dr. Grippe had long thought about the need for an alternative education program in Douglas County. So he and another teacher in the district cleaned out an abandoned mobile trailer at Douglas County High School and placed six middle school students in it. This was the first alternative education program in the county. It was named D.C. Oakes, after the man who started the Colorado Gold Rush. I will never understand why his name was chosen.

As the program grew, the district approached Swedish Medical Hospital to use the small building north of Castle Rock. The hospital wanted the district to purchase the building, but finally they settled for renting it.

The word got out that this school for " misfits" was going to be near their neighborhood, and they were very much against it. A meeting was held with those property owners, and Dr. Grippe promised them that there would be no problem with these children, and there never was. In fact for many years the students cleaned and maintained the road that went past many of their homes.

The first teacher to be hired for the program was Greg Simon, and a better person they could not have found. Greg had the academic background, and he had a personality that was a perfect match for these young people.

The program grew very quickly, and a larger facility was found in Castle Rock. When it reached 100 students, a second building was added in Parker. In 2003, the school was moved to the now vacant Philip Miller Library in the Plum Creek Center in Castle Rock.

Because of my background in Alternative Education, I became a close supporter for this school. I was very fortunate to have been able to award three $500.00 scholarships to graduates. One is now a teacher, one an EMT, and one has her own beauty shop.

Each year in January and again in June, graduation ceremonies are held at the school. Each student is required to speak to the audience and share his or her experience with this program. I tell you, there is not a dry eye in that auditorium.

The real success of our D.C. Oakes High School program can be attributed to the teachers who have worked there. These men and women are a very special breed. Do all of the kids at this school succeed and graduate? Of course not, but that number is very low. Whether they succeed or not, they will all tell you that, at least they had the opportunity to do so....something they had never done before.

EAGLE ACADEMY

In spite of the success of D.C. Oakes, Dr. Grippe believed that there was another group that needed our help. Those were the kids who had already dropped out and did not want to go the D.C. Oakes way. These boys and girls had jobs and could not hack the work and the schooling they needed. So Pat organized a new school -

Eagle Academy. It would operate in the late afternoon or evening and give the student a chance to earn their GED status. It was housed at Highlands Ranch High School, and today that program has been a lifesaver for hundreds of kids.

When people rate the Douglas County schools, they often brag about our CSAP scores, SAT and ACT scores, graduation rates, wonderful staff, and of course, our state champion sports teams.

But it is really the choices we give parents and schools like D. C. Oakes and the Eagle Academy that really set us apart from any other school district in this country.

COUNTY TOWN..A PIECE OF THE PAST REMAINS

County Town began with the wonderful book by Susan Appleby, "Fading Past,The Story of Douglas County." From her book I began to make yarn pictures of the places she describes in that book. When I bought my new home in 2004, I decided to build those buildings that I had made pictures of. And that was the creation of County Town.

The purpose of County Town was to help the children and adults to learn about the history of this very fascinating county. In the first two months over 800 children and adults came to County Town, along with several senior groups and friends.

When I decided to make a building, that structure had to tell a story. These stories came from Susan's book and my own research. Each story was printed on a board that was located behind the building.

Some buildings were made in a very short time, while others took much longer. The Cantril School and the old Courthouse that was destroyed by fire took over 3 weeks to build. That was because of all of the windows. Windows also added a great deal to the cost of the building. There was something going on in each building and they helped to tell the story. In the Victor House in Sedalia, there was a wedding taking place in the upstairs. At the Dry Creek Ranch, the men were making Limburger cheese. There was always that cheese for the children to smell. It was those features that made County Town so unique.

In this booklet you will see pictures of the Cantril School in Castle Rock and the 20 Mile House in Parker.

In January of 2005 I was diagnosed with prostrate cancer. The cancer was cured, but it left me so weak that I could no longer maintain the house. We sold the house in June, but now the question became. "What do we do with County Town?"

Thanks to our superintendent, Dr. Jim Christensen had many of the buildings moved to the Cantril School building. In time they will become a part of a historical museum in that building.

The Sedalia Historical Society bought several of the buildings from their area. I am so pleased that children will still be able to come and see the remnants of County Town.

Pictured on the following page are two of the buildings that were a part of County Town

20 MILE HOUSE..PARKER

The 20 Mile House was a stop over on the stage line for people heading for Denver.

CANTRIL SCHOOL.

This building was built in 1897 to replace the old high school that was destroyed by a fire. In 1984 it was placed on the National Register of Historic Buildings.

WHO WILL "MAN THE STORE" IN 2015

One of the goals of the No Child Left Behind Act is to have all students be proficient in reading and math by 2015. While this would be a laudable achievement, it is foolish to believe it will ever happen. No society in the history of the world has ever had that level of literacy.

Any student who ever took a course in Sociology knows that all societies must be composed to those who need a high level of academic talent and those who will never need that level of education. We will always need the engineers to design the highways, and we will always need those people who will pour the concrete. We live in a world that has reached the highest level of technology, and we live each day with gadgets that didn't exist even five years ago. But even with my PhD and years of schooling, I still have to pay $50.00 and hour to have my computer repaired. It costs double that when my toilet is stopped up.

I could be tarred and feathered if I said that, "We must always have a portion of our society that is willing to do the dirty work, and that will be done by the uneducated or poorly educated who will do those jobs." And that usually falls on the Blacks or other minorities. During my lifetime I have been able to observe how society has managed to develop and enlarge the chasm between the rich and the poor. In addition, I have seen how the make-up of that poor population has changed.

Abraham Lincoln once said, "Common looking people are the best in the world; that's the reason the Lord made so many of them."

President Bush would probably change that to "poor

63

people are the best in the world; that's why we are making so many of them." In 2000, the year before King George took office; there were 6.4 million families living in poverty in this country. Today it is 10. 2 million.

Back in Quincy, there were very few Black families. A few worked in the factories, but while the wages were good, they were not allowed to live in the nicer homes. As a result there was only two schools in that town that had any Black children.

The only Black person I saw in Quincy was the old man who operated the elevator in the department store. He reminded me of Uncle Remus with his white short beard. I don't imagine he had much schooling, but I would also bet that he was a pretty intelligent person. It was a pity that he had no place to show it.

Now that I live in Colorado, I will never see a Black person operating an elevator. That task is now in the hands of the Latinos. We know that less than half of the Latinos will graduate from high school. An even larger number will not even finish ninth grade. And why???? A non-graduate or drop- out can make enough money doing jobs that no-one else will do to make his car payment and live in an apartment.

Those people who want to close the borders or send those who are here back home better take a second look. Politicians will never admit it, but this country needs poor people and poor people are generally uneducated minorities. Poor people benefit Social Security; poor people help decrease inflation; poor people help to discourage immigration. Who wants to migrate to a place that is so poor?

Most of the legislation passed by Congress is designed to make the rich richer and the poor poorer. If you doubt that just count the lobbyists and the salaries they earn to make that happen. Count the "pork" that was in the recent Highway Bill. It doesn't take 15 million dollars to build a bridge to a place where no one lives.

I am in favor of every child doing the best he or she can do. But I also know that every child in America will not be able to reach that level of proficiency by the year 2015. There will always be those who are the underachievers, and we will always need them. I would like to see 100 percent improvement among the Blacks and Latinos. But that will never happen because our society will never allow it to happen.

Today, in Colorado, one in four college freshmen must take (remedial) courses to remain in school. This is at a cost of $15 million dollars. Thirty percent of our ninth graders never graduate. Colorado ranks 40th among states in spending per pupil and 48th in state support for higher education.

That pool of students who will be proficient by 2015 and will probably graduate from college have some real challenges that face him or her. What they have to look forward to is that students from India will be answering the phone in New Delhi to repair your computer.

Colorado is doing a fairly good job educating the children in elementary schools that do not have economic problems. We fail miserably at the high school level.

Those who have that lofty goal of all children becoming proficient in reading and math by 2015 better step back and really think things through. You may end up getting more than you wish for.

HOW SPECIAL IS SPECIAL EDUCATION?????

Most people don't know what the largest and most costly program we have in our schools. It has been called "Special Education" or often referred to as "Programs for Children with Special Needs".

I first learned about this special program back in 1957 when I began my teaching career. I was in the only building in the district that has programs for children with special problems. Most of these were physical in nature and children in wheel chairs. There were only five children in the district who had been identified to meet the criteria for the program, and they were all housed in this school.

The program consisted of teaching them in special rooms by a special education teacher. The idea of integrating these children into regular classroom was never even thought of. There was a sixth grade student who was legally blind who did come into my classroom at the end of the day to wait for his bus. Although he was legally bind, he could always see the clock (at 3:00) when it was time to leave and catch that bus.

It was in the late 1950's that the state of Illinois began to fund programs for special education. Categories were named and procedures for identifying and testing these children were developed. Many people were not in favor of housing these children in regular schools, and there was little support for having these children in a regular classroom, even for short periods during the day.

The first result of this special education legislation was the increased number of "discipline problems" who seemed to meet the criteria for placement. In the larger cities, this group was primarily Blacks and other minorities. The new laws, plus a multitude of court cases opened up the door for larger numbers of children being placed.

While there were classes for these children, they tended to be housed in self-contained classrooms. They were taught with very little concern for academic success. The most widely used educational tool in the room was a box of crayons. Again, as the programs grew there was a constant increase in the placement of minorities, especially black children.

In the 1990's, a new phenomenon appeared on the scene. That was the increase in the number of children who were identified as having "Learning Disabilities". Being a poor reader was not due to intelligence, but rather to some other physical trait that was causing this deficiency. It could be eye dysfunction or maybe it was a new term, "dyslexia". More and more research was showing how this new disability was causing so many learning problems. But again, the teachers were not yet on the scene to really use the new techniques that had been discovered.

Another thing that was happening in our school was the large number of children who were identified as having behavior disorders. These were children who were acting out in classes and being disruptive. We had always handled that problem with punishment. Now the doctors of America turned to a new drug, "Ritalin". At first, parents loved this treatment because it took the problem off their hands. But as more and more was learned about Ritalin, the use of it decreased. In the school where I was principal, we were dispensing Ritalin to over 20 children a day.

There was no doubt that special education was needed, and millions of children have benefited from it. But it is expensive. In this year's Federal budget 7.5 BILLION dollars was allocated for the programs. In Colorado over 107 million dollars is spent on these children.

While many parents and teachers object to this amount of dollars being spent, very few will ever publicly object to it. Some teachers still have to listen to children screaming in their classrooms. But I think they handle it very well.

Special education has helped many children, but perhaps those who benefit most are the regular children who have learned compassion and patience from their presence. I think that many parents have learned the same lessons.

THE TOWN BAND

EVERY SUNDAY AFTERNOON, THE TOWN BAND WOULD PRESENT A CONCERT IN THE PARK. THE BAND ALSO PLAYED FOR THE ANNUAL FOURTH OF JULY PARADE.

MOST OF THE MEMBERS OF THE BAND GOT THEIR MUSICAL TRAINING IN BANDS DURING THE CIVIL WAR. THE BAND PLAYED MANY KINDS OF MUSIC, INCLUDING HYMNS, WALTZES, AND MARCHES. BY THE END OF THE 1800S, JOHN PHILLIP SOUSA BEGAN TO WRITE MANY MARCHES, AND THESE WERE ALWAYS THE FAVORITES OF THE CROWDS. THE MOST FAMOUS MARCH WAS THE "STARS AND STRIPES FOREVER".

CASTLE ROCK TOWN BAND..AN IMPORTANT PART OF MY LIFE.

From the day my father bought me a trumpet in fourth grade, music has been a very important part of my life. It was the center of my life all through high school. It added to my U.S. Navy experience by playing in the various dance bands at the naval bases. For the next twenty years playing for dances put a lot of meat on the table for my growing family.

When I moved to Colorado, the horn gathered dust until one day I read in the local newspaper that a band was being formed in Castle Rock, and they wanted interested old worn out musicians to join it.

In 1998, Kent Brandebery, a retired music instructor in Douglas County Schools, organized a Town Band. It was patterned after the original town band of the 1890's. The uniforms even replicate those worn by the first band. I answered the call and became a member of the Town Band.

The band plays for a variety of occasions. We marched in the County Fair parade for many years. We help to light the star in November that sits atop the rock. During the Spring and Fall you will find us playing for concerts in our new Gazebo in front of the new Library.

We are not a high performing band. We play for the fact that we just love to play. We practice only two evenings a month, and those are a friendly social event, as well as grinding out those new tunes.

This is another classic example of how one person like Kent Brandebery can make a big difference in the lives of those he touches.

CHILDREN HAVE CHANGED..BUT HOW? WHY?

I entered this world on July 24, 1928 in a normal delivery. This means that I was a Great Depression baby, joining millions of others in that category. By the age of one, I was the son of a single-parent mom who had divorced my abusive Father. I don't know the details of how that all came about, as my Mother refused to ever tell me.

My Mother had to work to support us, so I was raised by a man and woman who lived in our apartment complex. They were truly wonderful people. He was a school teacher and the lady did not work. It is rather ironic that when I returned to complete my college degree, I did my student teaching requirement with him.

By the time I entered first grade, I had been subjected to living the life of a "Depression Child." We were very poor but really didn't know it. In fact I never learned I was poor until President Lyndon Johnson identified me as a member of the "Great Society". We thought that everyone hung out their laundry, and that applying new rubber soles to your existing shoes was how the world lived.

When I was four years old, my Mother re-married a very wonderful man. He worked for a drug store and was there seven days a week, ten hours a day. He also played the drums in a dance band that played on the ferry boat between Rock Island, Illinois and Davenport, Iowa. My Mother also worked as a waitress on that boat. So many nights they would take me along, and I would sit on the edge of the band stand and listen to this music. Is it any wonder that now, at age 77, I still play in a band.

Because my new Dad had to work many long hours, I was raised by Mother. She was the best softball pitcher on the block, and she and I shared many hours of listening to the Chicago Cubs baseball games on WGN radio and to the "big bands" from the Aragon and Trianon ballrooms in Chicago.

As a child, I don't ever remember knowing if any of my friends were rich. None of my friends ever had cars, we all pretty much dressed alike, and there were not many things for kids to buy. I do remember that one day I heard that one of my girlfriend's Father earned $10,000 a year. I made that my life's goal, but gave up that goal when I became "Just a Teacher."

There was one other way to know if a family was rich. We played a lot of softball and baseball. There was no such thing as Little League, so we had no uniforms. We just got the gang together and played. But the kids who brought the balls and bats must have been from the rich family.

After sitting on that bandstand for many years, my father decided when I was in 4th grade that I should play an instrument. He was also at that time getting tired of hauling his drums in his very small car. So, he sold his drums and bought me a cornet. It was purchased from the Montgomery Ward catalog for $34.00.

In those days, you could not be in the school band unless you were good enough to read and play the music. So I had to take music lessons for an entire year to get into our grade school band. My teacher was named Mr. Fraker. He was a big man who looked like he was a member of the German Army. I was not allowed to read and play any popular music. I had to concentrate on scales and breathing. All of that for 25 cents a lesson.

I became a member of the band in fifth grade, and I also became the drum major. This was during World War II, so we marched the draftees to the depot. It was about a mile, and we marched in all kinds of weather. I later became the drum major in the junior high school band and in the high school band when we moved to Burlington, Iowa.

In the junior high school band, I had two twin boys who marched behind me and twirled their batons. Many years later one of the boys played third base for the New York Yankees, and the other became manager of the Chicago Cubs.

In 1944, my father was transferred to Burlington, Iowa where he became the manager of the Walgreens Drug Store there. I don't know why, but in those days the condoms (or rubbers) as we knew them were kept in a locked drawer behind the counter. This was also a time when many items were rationed. People could not buy many things like women's nylon hose, cigarettes, and gasoline. My Father had a thing going where he would trade nylons with the man in the store across the street who had cigarettes and liquor.

When I was told in ninth grade that we were going to move to Iowa, I thought my life had ended. I was madly in love with Madie Jane Johnson, and I could not live without her. But since I enjoyed eating and living in a house, I gave in and moved with the family.

Strangely enough by the end of the first month in school I had completely forgotten Madie Jane and was madly in love with another girl. During my junior and senior year I went steady with Lucy ____. She was the daughter of the richest family in town. In those days, when you took your girl to the movies or a dance, the boys always paid the bill. I guess that is how girls get rich. But when I went off to the Navy and she went off to school at St. Mary's, Notre Dame, that romance ended.

My friends in high school were good people. We didn't drink alcohol, we didn't dress like we were from another planet, and no one had a ring in his or her nose or tongue. In fact we shunned any girl who smoked. Dating a girl who smoked was like kissing your brother.

When my high school class graduated in 1948, most of us went into the military. I don't know why we went, but I do think the G.I. Bill had a lot to do with it. For serving for two years, one could receive a paid college education. I am not sure, but I think that most of my friends were the first generation to ever get a college degree.

While this was a noble goal, it did create a very new and different generation of young people. Those college graduates now had a good paying job, and many now owned a home of their own. This created a generation who was obsessed with providing a better life for their children. This now became the "gimme, gimme, gimmee" generation. The parking lots at high schools became filled, and the new drug generation was created. The chasm between the rich and the poor was widening.

Life was not dull for these kids. Sports, cheerleading, dancing, gymnastics, Little League, and "pot parties" ruled their lives. This was the beginning of the "self governing-generation" because the parents were too busy making money to support all of these activities, or spend time with their children.

This was also the first generation of moms who entered the work place. Women first got a chance to work in those defense factories and they loved those big pay checks.

This was the first generation of young people who were told that they MUST go to college. How you earned that right I am not sure, but the pressure on kids to do well was intense. Cheating became a way of life for most teenagers.

When I began teaching in 1958, most schools were very well organized places of learning. In the school where I worked, the most violent thing we had was three boys arguing over the use of the slide rule during recess, (remember these are sixth graders). About 70 percent of the children in this school were Jewish and very well-to-do. They had a strong desire to do their best, and this seemed to motivate the others.

In 1963, I was assigned to my first school as principal. Now, for the first time I was going see just how the other half lived. This was the half who never benefited from President Johnson's Great Society. When I later moved to Galesburg, Illinois, my eyes were really opened. This school was composed of very poor and mostly Black students. These children became the generation that was very poor, jobless, rampant users of drugs, and an anger that was ready to explode. And as you know, it did. The big cities of Detroit and Los Angeles suffered the most, but it tricked down to every classroom in America.

Today, our classrooms are filled with the children of the "Baby Boomers." In the past ten years, the rich have gotten richer and the poor have gotten poorer. We have a society where every child must have a cell phone, personal computer, a camera that no longer uses film, just a tiny chip, and where the vast majority of teen-agers have their own credit cards. The economy is now dominated by what teenagers buy.

The children are involved in activities that are held each day of the week, Monday, singing lessons; Tuesday, Art lessons; Wednesday, Church activities; Thursday, Little League practice; Friday, Little League game; and on Saturday the Little League and Soccer games.

Children are rewarded for participation, not accomplishment. My grandson plays on a Little League team that has never won a game. And yet, he has dozens of trophies on his dresser.

In Douglas County, a new car on a 16th birthday is expected as a right of passage. We also bury many kids each year who had no respect for themselves or their peers when behind the wheel of that automobile. Our school parking lots look like "Rocky's Auto".

Today we have millions of young people who are attending colleges. They are consumed in alcohol, sex, and drugs. It takes many five or six years to get a degree, and the business world tells us how they see these young men and women. They live for the present, have no ways to deal with long term planning, expect constant praise for attendance rather than for accomplishment. They want "big business trophies" on their dressers for the same reason my grandson has his.

Every generation says that the present generation is "going to hell in a hand bag". The difference is that this generation's handbag costs $200, and it was charged on a Master Card that was owned by the teenager.

WE ALL NEED SOME CULTURAL SHOCK NOW AND THEN

In another part of this book, I mentioned that I had earned a sizable amount of money for writing the new Silver Burdette 7th grade Geography textbook. This money allowed my wife and me to take two trips to Europe and a fantastic journey to East Central Africa.

It is not my intent in this essay to describe in detail the experiences we had on that trip, although a few will be included. Rather it is to share the concern I have that most teachers will never be able to meet and share time with different cultures.

In the 1980's, teachers could deduct all of their expenses on their income taxes. Your dining room was your office, and all those expenses you all make now for supplies in your job were deductible, and so were trips like we took.

Many of my fellow teachers did take trips to Europe and other places. Most brought back pictures and slides of their trips to share with their students. Yes, the 700 slides I took in Africa were a tax write-off.

I am writing this because I believe that the elimination of those tax deductions have really had an impact on teaching in our schools. If teachers take trips today to foreign countries, very few come in contact with different cultures. A visit to Australia or Denmark is like visiting Chicago.

Our first trip to Europe was in 1972, when we attended an educational conference in Amsterdam. After three days of meetings, we rented a car (a Simca convertible) and took off for ten days. Since I am a trained geographer and my wife is a Sociology major, we spent a lot of time in the country side and small towns.

We first traveled to a small town in Northern Netherlands where the town was having a cheese market. The cheese is graded and selected by the buyers. The streets were filled with many of the people dressed in their Dutch dresses. The men were wearing their wooden shoes, and customers were eating raw eels. This is the part of the Netherlands where we find the tulips and cheese and the windmills.

From there, we headed for the city of Berlin. Since many of you were not around after World War II or know much about it, let me fill you in.

At the end of the war, Germany was divided into two sections. One was West Germany, occupied by the Allies, and the other was East Germany, occupied by the Russians. In addition, the city of Berlin was divided in the same way. The city of Berlin was divided by a large brick wall, known as the Berlin Wall. Its purpose was to keep the East Berliner from entering West Berlin.

The first thing you notice about Berlin is that much re-building is going on to repair or replace the terrific amount of damage that was done by the American and British bombers.

As you drive down the main street of Berlin, you come to a blockade and the sign reads "ACHTUNG. VER-BOTEN" (attention, you are forbidden to go past this sign). You were now facing that Berlin Wall, and you plainly see the guard post on the Wall, and each is manned by a German soldier with a machine gun pointed right at you. Although I had read about the Wall, I never got the true meaning of what it meant to those people in Germany who lived on both sides of the Wall.

Germany is a beautiful country, but the other thing that left its mark on me was the lack of men in the fields. This is what the loss of over one million men during wartime can do to the rural population.

We flew out of Rome to Nairobi, Kenya and the East Central part of Africa. The first thing that you learn about Africa is its immense size. You can place five United States on the continent of Africa. It took us as long to fly from Rome to Nairobi as it did to fly from New York to Rome. In Africa, all airports are "International" airports, even though most are smaller than Centennial Airport here in Colorado. We taxied down the runway and came to a stop just short of the fence. When I looked out of the window, I was staring into the eyes of a giraffe.

This was August of 1979, and Kenya had won its independence from Great Britain. But remnants of that colonization appeared everywhere. The money was British, and the countryside was dotted with the small farms that were broken off from the British plantations. In the city the shops were all Indian (from India), and the barter system was everywhere. No one ever paid full price for anything.

Our first outing was to Mt. Kenya, about 100 miles North of Nairobi. Here we could see the different crops on the hillside - corn, beans, tea, coffee, and the cinchona tree. This is where we get quinine.

After the trip to Kenya we headed South to Mombassa on the Indian Ocean. From Nairobi to Mombassa it is about 500 miles, and there was only one paved road. It was built during World War I. From Mombassa we had to fly to Zambia in order to come back into Tanzania. The border was closed between the two countries since they were not speaking to each other.

One doesn't have to be in Tanzania very long to see the dramatic differences between these two countries and their culture. Tanzania was a German colony, and even after freedom, Tanzania became a very strict communist country. There was no bartering in these shops. Again, there were few paved roads.

Tanzania is the home of the Serengeti Plain, a land area about the size of Texas. But on it are only two lodges and all dirt roads.

When I returned to the states, I was a very different person than when I left, and that difference became very apparent in my classroom. I had taken over 700 slides, and they became the foundation for the unit on Africa that I wrote. I realize that Kenya is not a typical African country, but it is an example of how a country can create an entirely new system of life from what they had.

I believe that any trip a teacher takes to a place that has a culture different from ours will make a difference in that teacher's classroom. It is very sad that the IRS doesn't feel trips for teachers is as valuable as golf outings in the business world.

THE SILVER BELL AWARD...
THE EDUCATION HALL OF FAME

During my forty-eight years in education, I have taught in 10 schools and been the principal of four elementary schools. I have worked with the best of the best and the worst of the worst. But in all of those years I was instrumental in only three cases to get a teacher removed from the classroom. I know that horrible is not a legal term, but these three people were horrible.

In another essay in this book I wrote that selecting a "Teacher of the Year" was a joke. But now I am going to deviate from that position and name the ten educators that I consider to be the best of the best during my 48 year tenure. All have either retired or are deceased, so I have not included any of the people I am working with now. I am also not including central administration people. Teachers, secretary, or principals make up my list.

In Cooperstown, New York there is the Baseball Hall of Fame. In Canton, Ohio there is the Football Hall of Fame. In Highlands Ranch now is the Education Hall of Fame. None of my recipients have set home run records or number of passes completed. My people have just set themselves apart from all of the people I have worked with by their dedication and the impact they have had on those around them and on me.

On the shelf of a book case in my living room is a silver bell. It is about three inches high and badly tarnished. It was presented to me in 1970 at our school Christmas program at Steele Middle School in Galesburg, Illinois. The children gave it to me because they knew that "Silver

Bells" was my favorite Christmas song. In all of my change of addresses, this silver bell has been my most cherished item, so I am going to use it for my Education Hall of Fame trophy.

I am also going to send complimentary copies of this book to each of these recipients.

SILVER BELLS AWARD LIST

1. **JIM JACOBS.** Jim was a fifth grade teacher at Nielsen Elementary School in Galesburg, Illinois. He has received many awards for his outstanding teaching at that school.

2. **DR. DAVE BEBELL.** Dr. Dave retired from his position as Principal of Eagle Ridge Elementary School in Lone Tree, Colorado. He was a teacher and administrator in this district, and he has left his mark on this county.

3. **JEAN SHUMARD.** Mrs. Shumard was the secretary at Steele Middle School and later moved to Galesburg, High School. In the 15 years she was my secretary, her loyalty and efficiency was totally "awesome." She still remains one of my dearest e-mail friends.

4. **BETTY ALTERS.** Betty was a fourth grade teacher at Steele Middle School for many, many years. Betty's room always looked like it had just survived a huge hurricane. But while her room was total chaos, her heart was not. She touched children in ways that most people never would.

5. **BEN Mc ADAMS.** Ben began his teaching career in fifth grade across the hall from me at Eugene Field Elementary School in Rock Island, Illinois. He later on became a Superintendent and completed his career as Director of Special Education in Moline, Illinois.

6. **BOB MEEHAN.** Bob was a special education teacher at Steele Middle School. He later on became the head teacher at the Alternative High School in Galesburg. He recently retired from his position as principal of Ogelsby, Illinois, Elementary School.

7. **JANICE PRAHL.** When I became a part of the Senior Volunteer Program, I was assigned to Janice (then Long) Prahl at Acres Green Elementary. She later on became a part of the Discovery (gifted) program, teaching 2-3 grade classes. She is now retired and wears the gold wrist bracelet that I wear as a Cancer survivor.

8. **ELIZABETH (BETSY) RINEHART.** Betsy was a teacher at Nielson Elementary School, and then later became the principal of Silas Willard Elementary in Galesburg. Betsy was the district's union leader (GFT) not GEA.

9. **ADRIAN BOOK.** Mr. Book and his wife raised me as a child in Rock Island. It was quite unique that when I did my student teaching at St. Ambrose, I was allowed to work with him as my critic teacher.

10. **MR. JOYCE DOUGLAS.** First of all Joyce is a man, and he was a fellow principal with me when we opened

the five new Middle Schools in Galesburg. He was a man who would not make most people's Hall of Fame because of the "silent influence" he had on so many people.

As I stated when I began to compile this list, it would take another complete book to describe why these ten were selected over hundreds of others. But, believe me, those qualities do exist, and I would be glad to share them over a cold glass of lemonade.

SECTION THREE

TESTS, TESTS TESTS

You were my girl in calico

I was your barefoot, bashful bean

I wrote on our slate

"I love you so"

"WORLD CLASS" NOT MEASURED BY TEST SCORES

If you have lived in this district more than ten years, you will remember the push that was designed to have Douglas County become "WORLD CLASS." It all began at a huge meeting at a hotel in Inverness where hundreds of businessmen, citizens, and educators proclaimed that someday our district would become World Class by the year 2000. This was the brain child of former Superintendent Dr. Rick O'Connell. This was also the beginning of the district's effort to become the very best it could become.

In spite of all of the hoopla, I never did find out if we ever became World Class. There was no celebration in 2000 that said we were now World Class. No buttons or banners were ever passed out. There wasn't even a sign put up on the Wilcox building.

What I do know is that we have the best damn school district in Colorado, and I believe we can rank with the best in the nation. I know this district is the best <u>bargain</u> on the market.

We have become that in spite of " C-CRAP" and the introduction of "Leave No Child Behind" from King George and his educrats.

A few people on Wilcox Street have attempted to measure World Class strictly by test scores. They believed that education was teach and test. Or is it more accurate to say "Teach *to* the test." They became this way by leaving the classroom and placing themselves behind a computer and a calculator.

As a Senior Volunteer, I get into several schools each

year. So, I will combine that with my 45 plus years in this profession to tell why we have the best school system in Colorado.

NUMBER ONE, PARENT INVOLVEMENT

When I walk into a building in this district, the first things I notice are the badges of the parent volunteers. They may vary in shape and style, but they tell me that parents in this school care about education, and they care about their children. Some read with little children; others help the older students with their math problems; most just become a friend who cares.

Many of these are not parents of the children. They are members of the Senior Volunteer Program. They carry out a lot of different duties, from sorting books to teaching classes in the classroom. Last year, volunteers were logged at 326,000 hours, worth 3.1 million dollars.

NUMBER TWO, THE WALLS IN THE HALLS

I can remember spending hours and hours outside of my classroom in preparing bulletin boards and typing and running off ditto sheets. In Douglas County, this work is done by a large number of paid teacher aides. They are the ones who make all of those things that cover the walls in the halls in our schools. Those aides are the most over-worked and underpaid employees in our schools.

These walls tell us what types of things our children are learning, and they clearly show what the emphasis is in our classrooms. There are pictures of families, trips the children have taken, and oodles and oodles of art projects. I recently visited South Elementary Schools, and there was art work in the "john".

NUMBER THREE, UNSTRUCTURED STRUCTURE

Most of you can recall what your classroom looked like when you were a student way back in PS #2. Desks, with initials carved in them, all lined up in rows and bolted to the floor. The teacher's desk was up front, with papers to grade on top of it, and the blackboards were filled with busy work and the names of the bad boys who would lose recess today.

In today's classrooms, we see small groups of children, stretched out on the carpeted floor, reading their favorite books. If you can't find the teacher, she is probably the tall one who is stretched out on the floor beside the kids. This is not chaos. I prefer to use the term "Unstructured Structure." Even the most physically impaired child is able to feel good.

The only thing missing from too many classrooms are members of the school board, and they don't know what they are missing.

Dr. Rick has now joined the ranks of us Senior Citizens. But I do want him to know that his dream of becoming "World Class" has become a reality. And that is based on what schools are all abut, CHILDREN, NOT NUMBERS.

CHANGES IN STANDARDS WILL AFFECT ALL STUDENTS

It seems like only yesterday, but actually it was six years ago that the Department of Education began to implement the new standards-based education here in Colorado. The original plan called for standards to be in place and tested the areas of Math, Science, Reading, Writing, History, and Geography.

I immediately volunteered to serve on the committee that would write the Geography standards for the elementary grades. We spent almost a year in doing this and finally had them in place. Then it hit the fan. The state decided that it could not afford to develop and test all of these disciplines, so they cut them back to reading, writing, and arithmetic.

For the past several years now, our children have become a laboratory for teaching kids how to take a test. Hours have been converted from the general curriculum so that more and more time is spent on just the three R's, and that is just the beginning.

Each year, more grade levels are added to the testing process, but nothing has been done about the disciplines that are not being tested.

As a teacher, I know how valuable the three R's are, and if a child can't read, there is no sense in putting him or her into other textbooks if they cannot be read. But let's face it, here in Douglas County the vast majority of our students are ready to move up to those other disciplines.

While the rest of the state waits for the inner-city students to catch up, which they are never going to do, our kids here have to tread water.

I am not suggesting that Geography and History are not being taught in our classrooms. They are. But there are only a few hours each day, and it can't all be done.

The reason the state doesn't begin to add those other subjects is simple. The state doesn't have the money to do so. The cost of giving and scoring the tests eats up the cost for new tests.

Many people would argue that Geography and History are not really that important anyway. The problem with that thinking is that the old type Geography of memorizing place locations is not worth that much. Our students will pay the price for this lack of maintaining the other disciplines when they reach high school, and these courses become requirements for graduation and entrance to college.

OUR LAWMAKERS JUST DON'T GET IT

One of the real faults of the democratic system of government is that too many of the people we elect have little idea of how the other half lives. These men and women (mostly men) are either from professions like law, teaching, and banking, or it's been a long time since they ever had to balance their own budgets or checkbooks.

There was an editorial in the *Rocky Mountain News* that stated the reason so many children in the inner- city could not read and score poorly on the CSAP tests, was that their parents don't take time to read to them. What a wonderful revelation that was.

What needs to be done is for these lawmakers and editorial writers to follow a working, single Mother for just one day and see what life is really like. They would see Mrs. Brown rising at the crack of dawn, getting breakfast and school lunches ready for her three children. Then she would probably board a city bus to her place of work that probably pays less than $10.00 an hour.

Mrs. Brown's children are probably responsible for coming home to take care of the siblings before Mom can get back home. In many cases, she will be home only long enough to go to her second part-time job so she can put food on the table. If she is lucky she will get home in time to put the older children to bed, then get ready to settle in for the evening to get ready for another day just like this one. Did you find any time in her schedule to read to the children? Maybe I missed it.

Another group of our lawmakers want to establish a voucher plan that will pay for Mrs. Brown to send her children to a better school. Those lawmakers who advocate the voucher system, say that Mrs. Brown is a prime candidate for a voucher.

There is no doubt that Mrs. Brown would like a better school for her children. That BETTER school is one where parents volunteer, children have their own computers, both Mom and Dad belong and come to the PTA meeting, and they always attend parent conferences. The Mothers in those "better schools" answer the phone when the teacher calls. Did you see a place in Mrs. Brown's schedule that would allow her to fit in to that environment?"

Each year when the CSAP scores come out, the children in Mrs. Brown's school do very poorly. The School officials start moving administrators around, get rid of those teachers whose classes did not score high enough, and threaten to put her school on probation. If you don't shape up, you could become a charter school. Wow! that ought to change that school into a "BETTER" school or else the state government will take over the school. And we all know what happens when state government begins to take over something. The only thing worse would be for the FEDERAL government to take over this school.

So if Mrs. Brown doesn't shape up and start reading to her children, even if it is eleven o'clock at night, she knows what can happen. The Bogey man won't get you, your local Congressman will.

WAD'JA GET...WAD'JA LEARN

It is not clear to me just when the first report cards were used in America. They seem to have been around forever. I also don't know _why_ report cards were even used in the first place. When I was in elementary school from 1932 to 1937, the A, B, C, D, and F were used on my cards. Thanks to my Mother's efforts she still had some of those cards until she passed away.

I always believed that an "A" showed you were smart, a "C" meant you were average, and an "F" meant you were a dummy. Back in 1932, we were allowed to use terms like "dummy". I am glad we did that because my good friend Jack would not be happy if he were "intellectually deficient." He really was a "dummy."

When I moved to Burlington, Iowa in 1944 where I attended high school, the ABC system was used. In those days high school was a social event. Most of the good teachers had gone off to war, and we were corralled with the left overs. Much of my time was spent in sports, band, and worshiping "Lucy."

When my report card came home, my parents always asked "Wad'ja Get?" Never did they ask, "Wad'ja Learn?" I think they cared what I learned, but they just followed what their parents had always said. "Wad'ja get?"

When I returned from my tour of duty in the Navy during World War II, I enrolled at St. Ambrose College in Davenport, Iowa, where all of my classes were graded with the infamous letters, A,B,C,D, and F. So I still had to deal with my wife then asking "Wad'ja get?"

Because of family obligations I had to drop out of school and go to work. When I decided to return six years later, the letter grades had not changed.

When I finally became "Just a Teacher" in Rock Island, this system used a very different grading system. It was S, N, U for school work, and 1,2,3 for discipline and effort. S was satisfactory, N was needs improvement, and U was unsatisfactory. A 1 was a good citizen, 2 needed to improve, and 3 was unacceptable. There was also two parent-teacher conferences a year.

It didn't take me very long to learn that a parent-teacher conference was a waste of time. So I decided to have the child at my conferences. The principal shook in her boots when she heard that, but she was afraid to say "No" because I was such a well respected teacher in this school.

In a traditional parent - teacher conference, the teacher tells the parents how the child has performed. If it is bad, then the parent goes home to find out why the grade was low. If it was the fault of the teacher, then now we had an argument between a parent and child. I also believed that if this was a good student, why not have the child there to hear all the good things.

When the child is present, we can ask the child, "Are you pleased with your good grade in math? You have worked so hard this term." You should see the eyes light up when praise is given.

When I first arrived in Douglas County, the ABC's were used. But now, that is going to change. Someone has decided that telling kids the truth is harmful to their growth. Since the new grades will only apply to elementary grade levels, the child and parent will only have to wait six years to find out if they have a "dummy" or not.

SEE The U.S.A. In Your CHEVROLET

"NO CHILD LEFT BEHIND"
RAISES MANY QUESTIONS

When George W. Bush ran for President in 2000, he promised to "Leave No Child Behind". The content of this Congressional Act was based on the reforms that President Bush made when he was the Governor of Texas. His appointment of Rod Paige as Secretary of Education was based primarily on his success as Director of Education in Texas. The Act was a 670 page document passed by Congress in December of 2001. At first, both political parties approved it, right along with apple pie and motherhood. After all, who could argue with a plan that was going to make a vast improvement in children learning? Since that time, the Act has been under constant criticism. In fact, the Governor of Utah, John Huntsman, signed a law that would ignore the provision of the law. The Federal Department of Education has threatened to withhold all Federal money from his state.

Let us look first at the provisions of this act and then what all of the hullabaloo is all about.

PROVISIONS OF THE ACT.

1. States are to create an accountability system to measure academic progress of sub-groups such as African Americans, Latinos, low-income students, and special education students to a state-determined level of proficiency.

Failure to reach these standards would end in punishment of those various kinds, from probation to the take over of a district by a local private firm. It also allowed parents in low performing schools to transfer their children to "better schools."

2. The NCLB act also requires that by the 2005-2006 school year, all teachers will be "highly qualified" as defined by law. A highly qualified teacher is one who has fulfilled the state's certification and licensure requirements.

* Possess at least a Bachelor's degree.

* At elementary level, the teachers must pass a test on reading, writing, math and other areas of basic elementary curriculua.

* At middle and high school, teachers must show mastery of the subjects they teach.

STUDENT TESTING

* Students will be tested annually in reading, writing, and math in grades 3- 8, and by 2008, all students in grades 3-5, 6-9, and 10-12 in science.

PARENT INVOLVEMENT

The state will issue an annual report card to all parents telling of the status of schools and districts. A parent must also be informed if a teacher who is not qualified is teaching their child.

PUBLIC SCHOOL CHOICES

School identified as needing improvement are required to provide students a choice of another school.

ARGUMENTS AGAINST NCLB

On the surface, it would seem that the goals of LNCB are laudable. The program wants teachers and students to be accountable for improving the performance of children.

There have been several criticisms of the program, but let me address just a few.

1. The program has not been fully funded as promised. Program dollars have been shifted from several existing plans, including Head Start.

2. Many rural and other small districts cannot afford to upgrade teacher in-service to meet the demands of certification.

3. Schools that have low-test scores and are placed on probation cannot find alternative schools for those who want choices.

4. Public education has always been the domain of local school boards. This is a huge step for federalizing public education. School Boards must now operate under the thumbs of the federal government.

5. It has been found that several school districts or teachers are cheating by elevating test scores and taking huge amounts of time to "teach the test."

Not only must the districts in Colorado meet the demands of LNCB, but also the schools are absorbed in trying to get good scores on the CSAP (COLORADO STUDENT ASSESSMENT PROGRAM) in the inner city schools, every minute is spent on teaching children how to take the test.

One of the major goals of No Child Left Behind is for all students to be proficient in reading and math by the year 2014. Now let us take a closer look at the goal.

1. Few of the legislators who passed this bill will be either dead or senile and still serving Congress.

2. In the history of humankind has there ever been a civilization in which all people could read and count.

3. The most dominant factor in low scores are the economic and cultural traits of the society. Do these lawmakers really believe that poverty and cultural attitudes will be erased by that year?

4. Why was this year, 2014, chosen? Does King George know something that the rest of us do not?

There has been some progress in raising test scores in many states. However, to achieve higher scores teachers will have to devote more time and energy in teaching kids how to test higher. For that, are higher test scores the goal of education or are there better ways to use that class time? I personally believe there are.

NEW WRITING PLAN WILL GAIN NOTHING

Here we go again. The blind are leading the blind.

Educators in Colorado, including those in Douglas County, are all in a tizzy about the writing test scores on CSAP. While our children score the highest in the state on the reading test, the scores on the writing section are much lower. As a result, the Board has passed new steps to correct the situation, and they are a joke.

To begin with, who ever set such a high priority on writing? In most of your lives, just how much writing do you do every day? Who really does any writing in life? Be honest, when did you do any writing to a friend or relative, not when you have a computer that types out what you have to say and makes the corrections for you.

Let's look at who does write. Of course authors do. Add to that free lance writers, journalists, advertisers, and those in business who do technical or business writing. So why was it so important for years for our kids to be subjected to this crazy idea of "Hole Language?" This approach told the kids to express themselves and don't worry about the spelling or grammar. If I followed that thinking, you would have trashed this book long ago.

Now we are toying with other ideas, and they won't work either. I am amazed that we are so surprised that our children can't write. First of all they are being taught by people who have never written anything in their lives. This is particularly true of elementary school teachers. Unless they graduated from a Liberal Arts University, they probably haven't had a course in writing in all of their schooling. Their writing experience has been writing a term paper that some undergraduate corrected, with very little follow up.

Writing is not a skill or even a talent. It is a PASSION. One has to be out of his mind to take the time it requires to express a series of ideas. Writers write to please themselves, not their readers. Once a book is published and someone buys it, the connection between the author and the reader has ended. My thrill in spending hours and hours to write this very short book ended when it went on the market for people to share my thoughts about several items.

Children can't write because they will never be in that position. When they write a story in class, who reads it? Do children ever get to share the wonderful experience of seeing their name on the cover of a book. The best a child can expect to get out of a writing exercise in class is a returned paper with red marks all over it or a letter grade.

I am a firm believer that a good writer must know and understand grammar. We quit teaching grammar many years ago because it wasn't any fun. I love grammar because I learned it by diagramming sentences, first on paper and now in my head. Unless you know the rules of grammar, you can't know if your are using them correctly.

Another problem that children have today is that they want to write it as they speak it, and you know what that can produce. Their vocabulary consists of like, awesome, cool, you know, and when you put those phrases to print, you end up with "garbage." Our kids are bombarded by people in the media who wouldn't know an adverb from a jar of pickles. There is nothing more dangerous than a "jock" with a microphone in his or her hands.

The Board of Education has proposed a five point plan to improve the writing scores in our district. 1) Collect date 2) Inform teachers) 3) Realign existing strategies 4) Provide teachers with assessment information 5) realign professional development. What in the hell is that all about? Never has there been a clearer example of "eduingo" by so many "educrats."

One of these district educrats stated, "Writing must be process driven, not product driven." This requires much discussion and practice. Who is this person trying to kid? If the state was not scoring writing for CSAP, we wouldn't even be having this conversation. The end goal of this new plan has the CSAP score as its product. It is the present and past processes that have screwed up the entire program.

People who write well do so for many reasons. For twelve years I wrote a weekly column in the Daily News Press. I never missed a deadline, and I never received a dime for it. I have also written three textbooks and a series of Historical Journals, and each time it was for the enjoyment it gave me.

One of the best teachers of writing in this district is Debbie Odom, grade 6 teacher at Castle Rock Elementary. If you want to improve your teaching of writing get a hold of her book *Writing Through the Tween Years*. Supporting Writers, Grades 3-6. This book was co-authored by Bruce Morgan, grade 3-4 teacher at this school.

We can't expect all children to like writing, especially if it is, *"My Summer Trip To Grandmas."*

Somehow, school officials forget what learning and children are all about. We are going wild testing and test results. Thank God we still have teachers like Debbie Odom and hundreds of others who are still putting children first. It is a secret we must protect and keep away from those in power.

Castle Rock Elementary teachers **Bruce Morgan**, grades 3/4 and **Deb Odom**, grade 6, co-authors of book entitled, <u>Writing Through Tween Years, Supporting Writers Grades 3-6</u>.

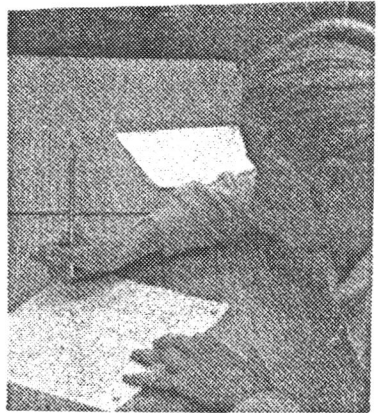

WHAT GETS TESTED..GETS TAUGHT

When CSAP first appeared in Colorado, several sessions were held with parents and community leaders to explain this new testing program. I am not sure what the real purpose of these meetings was, but they offered a free lunch, and I never turn that down.

CSAP was the new assessment (test) program designed to measure the proficiency of students in relation to the new standards that had been developed by teachers and CED staff. We were given samples of tests at various grade levels and asked to complete the questions. This was like trying to judge a cake contest by licking the icing pan.

Many of the opponents of CSAP argued that the tests are not fair to minority groups and to children with limited English language skills. This was the complaint of a Boulder teacher when he refused to give the test to his students. I would say that the tests that I completed in reading and writing would not be that difficult for any child who could speak our language and who could read at or just below third grade level and was a member of the middle class white race.

It has been my experience that poetry is especially difficult for most children to interpret. Much of this is due to the fact that they do not read much poetry in the lower elementary grades, and that it is taught very poorly. When you are fed a diet of "Old Mother Hubbard" and "Tom Tom, the Piper's Son" for five years, interpreting Gwendolyn Brooks in grade seven is quite a challenge.

When students in middle school are asked to identify how the poet has used "similies" in a poem, the teacher is now speaking a foreign language. Therefore, if teachers know that identifying similes will be on the CSAP test, they now spend hours making sure the children do well on the questions about "similes." I learned very early in my teaching career that "WHAT GETS TESTED, GETS TAUGHT."

I am not opposed to those students learning how to use similes in their writing. I am opposed to the amount of time that is taken to make sure the children will "test" very well. I would like to see some of that class time used to help children understand the implications of the First Amendment to the Constitution. Of course that will not happen because the state of Colorado is not interested in the Constitution and does not include American History anywhere in the CSAP program."NOT TESTED..NOT TAUGHT."

The CSAP program is very acceptable to most parents in Douglas County. It is one more source of "bragging rights" for the vast majority of our students and parents. Many educators use all test scores as the basis of the quality of education in a district.

When CSAP was in the womb stage, it was my understanding that these tests would be based on standards in all subjects. I can recall spending three years in committee meetings to write those standards. I wrote the standards for elementary grade Geography. I was so excited that finally teachers would begin to teach more geography than place location. I even held workshops for teachers in the district to learn how to do that.

But for six years now, not one question about geography has ever appeared on a CSAP test. The same goes for American or World History, Economics, Sociology, or any of those other "frill courses." If what is tested is taught, do the math. Incidentally, Math only became important this year, and now is tested and taught. Soon, Science will join the elite list.

The CSAP test will never challenge the abilities of our best students. The questions are written at a mediocre level of difficulty. Unfortunately, about one third of the children will never do well on CSAP. I personally believe that is one of the goals of many politicians in this state.

CSAP is an insult to the children and parents in this district and others like ours. Because what gets tested gets taught, our children are receiving much less time on the arts and social sciences. The difference between a child that is "partially proficient" and "proficient" is often one or two questions.

Most of the children in Douglas County are capable of handing the subjects like Geography and History. Unfortunately most are never asked to.

In Douglas County we have teachers whose head is not on the chopping block every day, and many of the subjects I am concerned about are getting taught and taught very well. The teachers I work with do an excellent job every day. It is those children in the inner city and rural schools that concern me. I only wish it concerned those "powers to be."

Our children could be better evaluated by the teachers who are teaching the children in our schools or by a test written at the local level that reflected what is being taught to our children. CSAP is diagnosing a heart condition by taking one's temperature as the only form of diagnosis.

TEACHER DEMONSTRATION IS A BIG HYPOCRITICAL JOKE

By now, you have seen the pictures and read the stories about the demonstration by the teachers in the Colorado Teachers Association. To me, a former teacher, this was a big joke and typical for teachers in that teachers union.

As long as I can remember, the National Educational Association has labored for "more money with less work". I first became a member of that organization way back in 1958, when it was still a professional organization. I remember the principal coming to me and telling me I had to join so our building could have 100 percent participation. At that time, the dues were only five dollars a year, but when I was making less than $50.00 a week, that was a lot of hamburger. When I said I could not afford to join, she stomped her feet and said she would pay my dues so we could be "perfect."

I remained a member for many years after that, until one year I was appointed to the negotiating team for the Galesburg Education Association. It was this experience that introduced me to the phrase " collective begging" to describe the way this organization bargains. The tactic was simple, ask the Board how much money they have, and then settle for that.

After that experience, I became a member of the American Federation of Teachers, and remained a member until my retirement. Since we were not the bargaining agent for our district, we had to live with the "collective begging" process for many years to come.

What this demonstration on the steps of the capital was all about was more money for less work. We heard that we need smaller classes, more supplies, more technology, and the list goes on and on. While they were justified in opposing this crazy new report card, behind the scenes it was all about MORE MONEY.

The hypocrisy of this event was that it was this same "union" that allowed the Governor to get his way and have the Legislature pass this bill. It was this same union that traded this legislation for the right to keep their tenure laws. Once again we saw where their priorities are when it comes to "collective begging."

To the credit of the Governor and the Legislature , funding for schools has increased dramatically during his time in office. If Jefferson County and the other districts would unload some of the fat that lives in the central offices, there would be more money. But when the CEA hears there is more money, their target becomes teacher salaries, with little going directly to the kids.

While Douglas County probably has the smallest central administrative staff in this area, they too seem to believe that every time we add a few students, we need to add some more administrators in the main office. We saw where their priorities were when the Board added an "Assistant Superintendent of Testing" instead of an "Assistant Superintendent of Reading or Math." Again, I remind you, "What Gets Tested, Gets Taught." And that is the direction we are going here in Douglas County and the rest of the state.

From the first day I was hired many years ago, I have opposed teacher tenure. I have seen too many bad teachers protected by the unions, a practice that is also followed in medicine and law. The good ol' boys take over, and there is as much a 'Wall of Silence' in education as there is in the police profession.

While the CEA screams for smaller classes, they almost always settle for more money in their pockets instead of those small rooms. The Governor claims that laws were broken by the people at Jeffco, but I am not sure that is correct. I just don't know for sure. I would have much preferred to see them demanding that the report card be based on improvement, instead of using the antiquated "Bell Curve" to give the grades.

The public long ago realized just what the objectives of the National Education Association are. They know that this organization spends millions of its members' dollars each election time to support people who believe in "more money for less work". After all, these politicians also work for a government. They make good bed-fellows.

TEACHER OF THE YEAR AWARD IS A BIG JOKE

Each year, hundreds of organizations conduct "TEACHER OF THE YEAR" contests. Almost all states do this for teachers and administrators. The recipient is presented with a certificate and sometimes a goodly amount of money. I can tell you from experience that this is not only an exercise in futility, but is also a dishonest activity and a joke.

In Douglas County, we have hundreds of teachers. I would say that most of them do a very good job with their children. I would estimate that about 10 percent should switch to selling Amway products where their talents don't harm the children. From the pool that is left, I would rate about ten percent as outstanding.

When I became a principal and was given the task of evaluating teachers, my criteria for being a great teacher was someone who taught as I did. I had problems with that teacher who ran a classroom like a zoo. I had the same problem with the teacher who worked for Sprint, where you could always hear a pin drop in her room.

I became the principal in a new middle school, grades 4, 5, and 6. In grades 5 and 6, the teachers worked in a departmental organization. That means that one teacher in each grade taught all of the Math. One taught all of the Social Studies, and one taught all of the Science. The children had Music, P.E., and Art with special teachers.

How in the world could you possibly select the best teacher from that group? Those teachers who taught the math classes had to have a mastery of that subject. The Social Studies teachers had to be judged more on their methods rather than content.

Several years ago, a teacher was picked as the teacher

of the year by this organization. When the TV station covered the story, they mentioned that she had her children "make globes out of paper-machete." Can you believe that? Socrates would have had his students do that if they would have had paper in his day.

It is a lot easier to name the "bad eggs" in the basket than it is to identify the good or even master teachers. It is a rare school when one teacher ever gets to see another work in their classrooms. Great teachers are often the loneliest people in a school.

Naming the teacher of the year is a real slap in the face to all of the other teachers. Most teachers laugh under their breath when one of their colleagues receives such an honor.

In 1983, I was nominated for the "Top Ten" award in the state of Illinois that selected the top ten elementary and secondary teachers in the state. The nomination process consisted of a fellow teacher submitting a folio of my teaching assignments, parent letters, fellow teachers' letters of recommendation. I was fortunate to win one of those awards, but I would have never been considered if that teacher had not done all of that work. The awards banquet was held in a hotel in Chicago with hundreds of people there. While the superintendent did grant me a personal leave day, he refused to pay for my meal (he is the one we fired at the first board meeting).

I really do wish there was some way to reward good teaching beside playing the game of "teacher of the year." If you come up with a method of doing that, let me know. I used to have a sign in my office that said, YOU DON'T HAVE TO BE THE BEST. YOU JUST HAVE TO DO YOUR BEST. It certainly applies to children, and its not too bad an idea for teachers.

EARLY RETIREMENT IS NOT WHAT
IT IS CRACKED UP TO BE

By 1985, I had decided it was time to leave education and move on to something different. For many Summers we had spent our vacations at a place called Cloud 9 Ranch in the Ozarks of Missouri. One year, I was asked to write the history of that Ranch. I collected stories about the people and events that happened on the Ranch when it was a 7000 acre lumber camp. It became a book called "The House on the Hill."

I so enjoyed this project, that when I returned to Galesburg, I contacted the local newspaper and asked if they were interested in publishing such a magazine about the history of the county. I became the editor and the sole reporter of the historical information. The magazine was called, *Prairie Journal* and was an instant success.

During the second year of the magazine, I was asked by the people to run for the Board of Education. The district was in a financial mess, and the people wanted to have the superintendent removed. Four of us ran on the platform to promise to remove the superintendent at the first meeting after the election.

The dismissal of the superintended created a lot of problems within the community. Many of the businessmen were friends of the superintendent, and they contacted the editor of the newspaper and cancelled many of their ads. Because of this, the owner of the newspaper cancelled the magazine.

At the first meeting of the School Board, we did give notice to the "Sup" that his contract would be terminated as soon as his replacement was hired. The Board members took a trip to Tennessee to visit with the community of our proposed new candidate to get the reaction of obtaining the new superintendent. He received the laurels and the commendation of the people. Little did we find out from a few people why that town was so glad to have him move on. His credentials were impeccable, and we looked forward to hiring our new superintendent.

It didn't take long for me to learn that a School Board was not a place for an ex-teacher. Let me share some of my early experiences.

Much of my first term was attending expulsion hearings. In the first month, we expelled over 22 students. I kept pushing for the district to develop an alternative school to help these kids. But in the end was a 5-2 vote not to give these kids any help.

At an early Board meeting, the Board was asked to approve a new English text book and student workbook. I had reviewed the material and found them to be very inadequate. The vote was 5-2 again in favor of the bad textbooks.

In the second term, the Board was asked to approve a request from one of the junior highs to purchase venetian blinds so the teachers could show movies and other audio-visual materials. During the meeting, there was a shift from the blinds to a request from the high school athletic department to resurface the track around the stadium. Again,

1. request to replace blinds, defeated 5-2
2. request to replace the blacktop on the track, in favor 5-2

This was really the icing on the cake for me. I was beginning to have headaches and felt that I was not serving the community. So I submitted my resignation. The vote 5-1.

It was also at this time that I was visiting local schools to become better informed. But when the new Boss heard of this, he said "No more of that. I will inform you of anything you need to know."

So far, I have told you the reasons why I resigned from my time on the Board. What I have failed to tell you is that the 2 of the 5-2 votes was a former teacher. She loved the conflict. I DID NOT!

SECTION
FOUR

TEACHER'S PET

When

We

Were a couple of kids

NEW DOUGLAS COUNTY HIGH SCHOOL #8 WILL BE A COMMUNITY CENTER OF LEARNING

In 2006, a new high school will open in the Meadows of Castle Rock. But it will be like no other high school in this area. At the present time it is referred to as HS#8, but I am sure that in time it will have a name. You can't develop cheers around a number.

The school will open with 9th and 10th grades only. It will join other high schools across the nation that are joining the "Breaking Ranks Movement" for high school reform and structure. The school is more of an academy style (smaller learning communities) and focuses on becoming a true community and neighborhood school.

Dr. Lisle Gates is the new principal of HS#8. He comes from many years as the principal of Highlands Ranch High School. Staff members are currently considering partnership proposals and ideas from various community organizations. Meetings have been held to discuss how the facility can be used during non-school hours to provide adult education, arts, and cultural entertainment and neighborhood library use.

Sixteen core faculty members have been hired to head up the curriculum development and structure of the "academies". The new high school will be a strong academic institution with college connections for all students.

The tentative "academies" in this new liberal arts school may be centered around the Performing Arts, Math/ Science, Engineering, Information Technology, World

Language and Health Services. In addition, the school will have a strong athletic and activities program.

The school will be approximately 250,000 square feet, with two floors. Its enrollment will hold 1,600 students, and can expand to 2000 students.

Until its opening in 2006, the staff will be actively involved with the community. The community will be holding meetings to choose school colors, school's name, and mascot, etc. Dr. Gates is on duty each day, and he can answer questions you may have, his phone is 303-387-5492. His e-mail is lisle.gates@dcsdk12.org.

OLD ROUTE 66 IS STILL ALIVE AND WELL

Thanks to President Dwight Eisenhower the United States has the finest interstate Highway System in the world. Thanks to "IKE" we have Interstate Highways that run from South to North and numbered from I-10 to I-94 and from West to East numbered from I-5 to I-95. In addition there are many highways that circle the larger cities like C-470.

Those from my generation remember the earlier highways very well. Two lanes, stops in all of the towns, and many times very bumpy. I especially remember old Route 66. You may have never driven on route 66, but you learned about it from singers Nat "King" Cole and the Andrews Sisters.

"You go to St. Louis, Joplin, Missouri, and Oklahoma City is very pretty.

See Albuquerque, and Gallup, New Mexico,

Flagstaff, Arizona, Kingman, Barstow and San Bernardino."

When I was 10 years old, I went on vacation with my parents. We traveled from Illinois to Arizona to meet my Mother's brother. It took us three and a half days to travel 850 miles on Route 66. There was only two lanes, and we had to drive slowly through every town. There were no motels or Mc Donald's. You stayed in roadside cabins or hotels, and you ate in the local restaurants. Gas cost about 18 cents a gallon, but when you stopped for gas, an attendant came out and pumped the gas, cleaned the windshields, and checked your oil and tires. Remember that Route 66 ran across the southern part of the country, and these were the days of no air-conditioning. Cars did not even have directional lights. When you turned left or right, you used your arms out the window.

In September of 2005, I took a week off from volunteering, and took a trip to the West and the Grand Canyon. That trip involved driving on Interstate 40...the old route 66. What great memories that was. I had often flown over this area, but I wanted to see it from the ground.

I really enjoy driving cross country. I am a trained geographer, so I see things that most people don't see or care to see.

When I work with my geography classes, I teach them geography is:

"WHAT IS WHERE, WHY, AND WHAT OF IT."

Let me share some things I saw along the highway that most people never see. I will use the definition above.

1. About ½ of the country West of New Mexico is wasteland and desert. How is the land used, and what effect would this have on the people.
2. Over 90 percent of the rural population lives in trailers.
3. The vast majority of North Eastern Arizona is a Navajo Indian Reservation. How are these Indians using this land?
4. I never saw a two-story house in the rural areas Why?
5. Many of the homes in Albuquerque are adobe and built in the Indian or Spanish style.

Just inside Arizona-New Mexico are two National Parks: Painted Desert and the Petrified Forest. These were both breath-taking places. Traveling through here was the highlight of my entire trip. This area consists of 50,000 acres of geological formations that were formed 250 million years ago; the area was once the home of several different species of dinosaur.

The plan for day three was to drive to the Grand Canyon from Flagstaff. The lady at the motel told me of a train ride that goes to the Canyon. So I called the train company and got a deluxe reservation on the morning train. It was great. I had a seat in the upper observation car, and we had music, champagne, snacks, and on the ride back, we had a hold-up on the train.

I was really not impressed with the Grand Canyon. It is truly a "BIG HOLE IN THE GROUND," but it is so massive it is hard to get good pictures of it. As a part of the train ride, we had a bus tour of the rims and had dinner there.

If you ever plan to go to the Grand Canyon, take a tour or the train. It was not the big season for tourists, but it was packed, and people had to walk long distances from their parking lots.

On Thursday, I drove through the North-Eastern section of Arizona. This is all Navajo Indian reservation. It is a vast waste land. I drove through here about 3:30 in the afternoon, and there were school busses everywhere. I stopped and asked the Indian driver how far he had to drive on his route. He said 25 miles north of the school. There are several casinos in this part of the state, and all of the Indians benefit from the money rose at these gambling halls.

Along this road is the Park Canyon de Chilles (pronounced Shay). Here again the formations were just outstanding.

During my life time I have traveled to Canada and Mexico. I have been to Europe twice and to East Central Africa. I have been every state except Hawaii and Alaska. But whoever said, "There's No Place Like Home" must have driven on Old Route 66.

THE CHANGING ROLE OF THE PRINCIPAL
GOOD SCHOOLS = GOOD PRINCIPALS

In the early schools in Douglas County, the principal was the teacher, janitor, nurse, and disciplinarian. Teachers were adults who could read and write better than the kids. The women teachers were not allowed to be married. The donations from the Thanksgiving turkey and the Christmas ham far exceeded their monthly pay checks. No college education was required, but as time went on more credentials were needed.

When I was hired for my first teaching job, my contract contained the following:

1. Paid once a month for nine months. No Summer checks. 2 Base pay, $3200. This included $200 for each of my four children. I received no allowance for my fifth child. We called this a Presbyterian schedule and discriminated against Catholic families.

I became "Just a Teacher" in August of 1957, and I was assigned to teach Social Studies and Language Arts to a classroom of 34 sixth grade children at Eugene Field Elementary School in Rock Island, Illinois. Like all teachers, I will never forget that first day when 68 eyes stared at me. Here I was in MY CLASSROOM, with MY STUDENTS, and I was finally "JUST A TEACHER."

My principal was an "Old Maid' who came into my classroom every day just looking for something wrong. We had teacher meetings every Monday after school. At these meetings she read every item on the agenda. (Later when I did become a principal, I learned why she did this.) TEACHERS NEVER READ THE BULLETIN.

Another lesson I learned very quickly was that good teachers are lonely teachers. That is why schools have doors on all the rooms. Many teachers need that place to hide. I was later a principal in a school that had no doors.

I was not a traditional teacher. I individualized my reading program, developed a series of lessons on diagramming, organized a debate team, and we had College Bowl teams. I had many teachers from out of the district come to visit my classroom. One lady came one day and when she was leaving my room she said, "My, those children were LEARNING." I thought, isn't that why they are here? The walls of my room were covered. I even had footprints on the ceiling with prepositions on them.

Although I was a "god" to the kids and the parents, I was an ogre to the rest of the staff. But after about the third year, teachers began to come to me for ideas and help. I learned that many teachers wanted help, and they would not get it from an old maid who spent most of her day finding fault.

THE NEED WAS THERE FOR THE NEXT MOVE

About my third year in the classroom, I decided to go to Western Illinois University to work on a Master's Degree in Administration. I had to drive 70 miles, three days a week and spend two Summers on campus to obtain that degree.

In the Summer of 1962, I learned that there was going to be an opening in an elementary school for a principal. When I went to the Assistant Superintendent to pick up my application, she said, "I will give you an application, but I will tell you that we don't hire MEN and we don't hire CATHOLICS. (DO YOU REALIZE HOW MUCH THOSE WORDS WOULD BE WORTH TODAY?)

There were 13 women and me who applied. We were interviewed and screened by a group of ten teachers. And guess who got the job? ONE CATHOLIC MAN. This had to be the saddest day in the life of that Assistant "Sup."

In Rock Island, new principals had to start at the bottom of the tree. My first school was located on an island in Rock River. Two weeks after I took the job, the school was flooded and had to be closed.

My next assignment was at Lincoln Elementary School in downtown Rock Island. This school had been built in the 1870's. The children came from low economic families, except for a few who where children of Augustana College professors. I tried to have an un-graded reading program, but that failed because of the 80 percent turn-over of the students.

1967 was not a good year for me. While I was a very successful teacher and principal, I was a horrible Father. I became married to my jobs, and that ended in a divorce from my wife of 19 years.

In that year, I received a call from a superintendent to come to Galesburg, Illinois and become a principal of one of the five new middle schools. These schools were all new buildings, arranged in "pods," and housed grades 4, 5, and 6.

I was allowed to select my own staff, and that proved to be no problem. This school would consist of low income families, farmers children, and the highest Black population in the city. So the people who applied really wanted to serve this community. All of the third grade teachers in the predominately Black elementary school wanted to come to our new school.

The school was named "Steele Middle School" and was named after a former Superintendent. It was at this time that I met a teacher in my workshop, and we were married over the Christmas break.

TIME OUT TO FINISH NEW SCHOOLS

The new middle schools were to open in 1968, but roof problems caused a one-year delay. Therefore, the superintendent asked me to work at Cooke Elementary school. What a shocker this was to be.

This was the height of the racial problems in our country. The children in this school were allowed to run rampant. The sixth grade teacher had a paddle on his desk. He also allowed his students to play baseball all day if they behaved in the morning. Children were climbing in and out of the windows. It was a real challenge, but by the end of the year, things were back to normal.

Steele Middle School opened in the Fall of 1968, and would you believe, with a big problem. Children from one of our feeder schools who went to school in the country, came to a Board of Education meeting, and their leader told the board they would not come to Steele School. They wanted to go to the upper-class school in the north of town.

After a closed session, the board told the people that they could attend the school in the north, but there would be over 28 children in the classrooms, or they could come to Steele where classes would be much smaller. They chose the latter.

On the opening day of school, we had parents and children greet these rural students. I told the father that led the opposition.

"Mr._____, you can tell your daughter anything you want about Blacks, but it won't take her ten minutes in the classroom to find out you are a liar." In no time at all, these parents became the most supportive in our school.

THE LEADERS IN DOUGLAS COUNTY
ARE THE BEST

During my years in Douglas County, I have met and worked with some really fine principals. Most of these are now retired, but they left their mark on this entire school district for years to come. People like Dr. Dave Bebell, Gary Poole, Dave Minter, Edna Doherty, Dave Bradley, and many others who have left their mark on this district. In all of the years as a principal, I never had an assistant principal, not more than one secretary. No BRT's or counselors. The payroll in our district was done by one lady and without a computer.

The role of the principal now is that of a "manager" instead of an instructional leader. In one school, I counted this list of people who worked there:

Administration 3
Classroom teachers 35
Specials (art, music, etc.) 5
Librarians 2
Office staff 4
Custodians 3
Cafeteria workers 4
Education assistants 9
Volunteer coordinator 1
Special Education 5

Total   74 plus

This is why principals have to be managers. The wonderful thing about our leaders in this district is that they do the task, and THEY DO IT WELL.

HOW RACIST ARE OUR SCHOOLS?

If you ask most people, "are you a racist?" most would answer, "of course not." But do they know, in what forms does racism appear, especially in our schools?

In my growing up years, I came into contact with very few Black children. My elementary school years were spent in Quincy, Illinois where prejudice was rampant. Not between black and white, but between Catholic and non-Catholic. Students from the Catholic High School and the public high school even walked down different sides of the streets. One year the football game between the two schools had to be cancelled because of this friction of religions.

There were some Black families in Quincy, but housing laws kept them in one part of town. Consequently all of the Black children went to the same, all-Black schools. So it was not until many years later that those schools were integrated.

All of my father's relatives were from southern Missouri. So I often heard the word "Nigger" being used in their conversations. My Uncle Fred was a retired barber in Hannibal, Missouri. He was a great baseball fan of the St. Louis Cardinals and listened to the games on radio. He was hard-of-hearing and wore a hearing aid. But when Jackie Robinson and other Black players appeared with the Cardinals on the scene, my uncle threw away his hearing aid and said, "It is bad enough to see those Niggers on the field. I don't have to listen to those announcers talk about them."

When we moved to Burlington, Iowa in the 1940's, again I saw no Blacks. As in Quincy, housing pattern was the instrument of the racists.

In 1946, I joined the Navy and was sent to Great Lakes for "boot camp." We had only one black man in our company, but in less that a week, the men from the South had scared him out of our company. He was transferred to an all-Black company in Georgia.

When I returned to attend college in Davenport, Iowa the director of the band was a Black man, but he was the only Black teacher at that school. But I did become very friendly with a young Black man who was studying to be a dentist. We often walked home after classes. On more than one occasion, we were stopped by the local police, and he was asked what he was doing in this neighborhood. The irony of this story is that this man went on to the University of Iowa, did become a Dentist in Davenport and even served six years on the Board of Education.

When I completed my education at St. Ambrose, I was hired to teach sixth grade at Eugene Field in Rock Island, Illinois. This was an all white school, with a Jewish populaton of about 70 percent. It was here that I came upon a different form of racism.

At Christmas, the children put on a Christmas pageant. Or should I say a Christmas-Hanukah program. The songs and stories were about half and half. One of my non-Jewish Mothers came to me one day quite upset and said she did not want her daughter to participate in the program. She said, very emphatically, "Why do we celebrate the birth of one man and the people who killed him at the same time?"

When I was made principal at Lincoln Elementary, I wanted to have a Christmas program, and I included a second grade class singing a song about a Dradlel (a

Jewish top). I asked two of my second grade teachers to do this. One was a very lovely, older lady in her 50's and a lovely Christian woman who had been at this school for many years. She came into my office, and said very calmly and softly, "I will not teach my children about those people who killed my Savior." I couldn't believe what I was hearing. I complied with her wishes, and one of my third grade teachers agreed to do the song.

In the same year, we put up our house for sale. We lived in a very white Christian neighborhood of older families. One day the realtor came to show our home to a Black family. This man was a new professor at Augustana College and his wife was a registered nurse. But within an hour after the family left, we began to get those phone calls, "We don't want no niggers in our neighborhood." We were sorry that they did not buy the house, but I often wished they had. This was a family that would have changed a lot of minds. Or would they?

I believe it is hard for any white, Christian person to answer my initial question until some circumstance puts them into a position when they actually have to deal with it on a personal level. It is obvious that there is more racism than we want to believe there is.

CAN YOU PLAY A TRUMPET "BY EAR?"

Since I have moved to Colorado, I have become a great supporter of the Country Dinner Playhouse. Throughout the years, I have enjoyed Fiddler on the Roof, My Fair Lady, Do Patent Leather Shoes Really Shine Up, and Oklahoma. But my all time favorite is The Music Man. The music is exciting, the costuming fantastic, and the plot challenging. But the real strength of the play is its message, ALL CHILDREN SHOULD PLAY A MUSICAL INSTRUMENT.

My step father passed away before the play was presented, but he must have heard Professor Hill. When I was in the 4th grade, he decided he would sell his drums and buy me an instrument. He had played for many years with "Tony's Iowans" a small dance band. They played around town and on the ferry boat that crossed between Davenport, Iowa and Rock Island, Illinois. My Mother worked on the boat, and often they would bring me to work, and I would sit on the end of the band stand and pat my feet to the music.

My new step-father, Andy, wanted to know what instrument I would like to play. I said either a trombone or a saxophone. So I settled for a cornet. He ordered one from the Montgomery Ward catalog and my Mother arranged for me to take lessons once a week for 25 cents a lesson.

My teacher was named Mr. Fraker. He was a huge man and as bald as an eagle. He was very demanding and insisted on me practicing 20 minutes a day. He also forbade me from playing any songs on sheet music until I had mastered the fundamentals of good breathing and vibrato.

By the time I was ready to read sheet music, I had already mastered "playing by ear." This means that if you know how a tune goes, you can play it without music. I would play the horn with Harry James on records. He was my favorite. If you can play by ear, there is no reason to buy any sheet music.

In fourth grade, I tried out for the school band. In those days, lessons were not taught in school. I qualified for the band. In fact, I was also selected to be the drum major to lead the band in parades.

Each week, the men who went off to war marched from the enlistment office to the train station .The different school bands would take turns in leading the parade. One time, it was so cold that by the time we reached the depot, we had to thaw out our valves on the station radiators.

At the end of ninth grade, we moved to Burlington, Iowa. I immediately joined the band, and was also chosen to be the new drum major. The regular band director had not returned from the war yet, so we had a woman who filled in for him. In fact, she was so big, she could have filled in for a whole section of clarinets. I don't think she could read music, so I was given the task of arranging all of the presentations at the football game. Mr. Wright did return for my senior year.

We organized a small combo who could all play by ear. One night we played a "gig" at a roadhouse in Gulfport. It was a real dive. During intermission, a man came up to me and said he wanted to see my trumpet. I was too small to resist, so he took the horn, went to the bar and hit a man over the head with it. I had to rent a trumpet until my parents could afford another one.

When I finished '"boot camp" at Great Lakes Naval

Training Station I was shipped to Bainbridge Hospital Corps School. One of my classes was chemistry. On the first day of class, the teacher (also the dance band director) asked if anyone played an instrument. I told him yes, but I didn't think I had time to study chemistry and practice in a dance band. He whispered to me. " You play the horn, I'll take care of the chemistry." Can you believe I got an "A" in chemistry? To this day, I can't even mix bath salts and water.

Over the many years, I have played in two combos and one Big Band. I much prefer the combos because I can play "by ear". I do not enjoy reading notes.

Several years ago, when I was volunteering at Acres Green Elementary, the assistant principal organized a teacher's band. We played one night for the school board. This was the first and only teacher band in this district.

Today I play in the Castle Rock Town Band and really enjoy it.

So, if professor Harold Hill contacts you to buy your child an instrument - do it. But don't purchase a trombone...we already have 76 of them, and by all means, teach your child to "play by ear."

FREDDIE AND HIS RHYTHM KINGS

For twelve years, I played with this combo called "Freddie and His Rhythm Kings." We played for Belgium weddings and wakes, and we played for local lodges like the Moose and Elks.

In the 40's and 50's the big bands of Harry James, Benny Goodman, Glen Miller, and Tommy and Jimmy Dorsey kept the people dancing. But in the smaller towns it was local combos like ours that put out the music. You may notice that we never used a piece of music, and yet we could play anything the people wanted to hear. We all played BY EAR.

MY 50TH CLASS REUNION

In 1998, I attended my 50th class reunion in Burlington, Iowa. We had over 200 graduates there, one as far away as Argentina. At a class reunion it is easy to recognize the men because their faces look the same. It is their waistlines that are so different. It is not easy to identify the ladies. Neither their faces nor their waistlines have remained the same.

When I walked into the country club, a voice rang out, "Did you bring your trumpet?"

Yes I did, and I got to play with the small combo that was playing for dancing. Once again, my ability to "play by ear" paid off.

THE CHANGING ROLE
OF THE SUPERINTENDENT

Dr. Donald Davis was the Superintendent of the Des Moines, Iowa School District. He also held that position in Moline, Illinois and other districts. He was a man who could come into a district and truly make a difference. He once told me that the average tenure of a superintendent was about five years. He said that a good superintendent who was doing any thing would probably alienate 20 percent of the public each year, and in five years, he had lost them all.

That may be true in some districts but it has not been my experience with some of the "sups" I have worked for. Let me describe five of the superintendents that I have faithfully served. I will not use names because some of them are still alive.

#1. GRANDPA EARL

When I was hired in Rock Island, Illinois, I came into Grandpa Earl's district. He had been the boss for thirty five years, so he doesn't fit Dr. Davis' mold. This school district was a good district because of good teachers and good principals ("als" not "les") The school district was always on sound financial grounds because the business manager and the superintendent had not spoken to each other for years.

Visiting the superintendent was like going to confession. Earl always listened, and at the end, you wondered why you even bothered to see him. Everyone in the community just adored Grandpa Earl. In fact, a new school was named for him even before he retired.

#2. HIT THE TRAIL, ORVILLE

From the day he was hired, Orville____ had enemies. No one trusted him, and he had spies in all of the schools to keep him informed of the activities of the local union.

When he hired me from another district, he told me he couldn't pay me as much as I was making there. I told him not to worry because he couldn't pay what I was worth anyway.

But these things were not his down fall. Basketball did him in. In this town basketball was a religion, and the coach was the almighty. To add to his woes, his daughter was dating the star basketball player, who just happened to be Black.

In his third year as the superintendent, it was discovered that the coach was doing some things with the athletic funds. Add to that was the fact that he was also a physical education teacher, who couldn't seem to find the gym during the day. Finally, it became necessary for Orville to file charges and asked the Board to dismiss him.

This ignited the town like you wouldn't believe. Cars were driving around with bumper stickers saying "ORVILLE, HIT THE TRAIL." (Trail was his last name.) The crowds at the board meeting were as large as they were at the games.

Did I tell you that Orville did "hit the trail." The coach was re-hired and the four Board members who voted to fire the coach were defeated in the next Board election.

#3. GORGEOUS GEORGE

When Orville left town, the high school principal was appointed to be the Interim Superintendent. He was a great principal but a horrible "sup." But they appointed him on a conditional basis. We all knew that trouble lied ahead.

George knew every kid in his high school, and the teachers worshipped him. His problem was managing money. By the end of his second conditional year, the district was millions of dollars in the red. So much so, that the Board had to close eleven schools and dismiss 100 teachers.

The community was so enraged that the citizens asked me to run for the Board. I had just retired, and I won the election by the largest vote in our history. It was not that we were so loved, but rather we ran on the promise to fire George at the first Board of Education meeting AND WE DID. Our mistake was that we allowed him to remain on the job until we could find a new one.

It was interesting that when we tried to find a teaching position for him, he was not qualified to teach anything.

I should also tell you that the new Superintendent had women problems, and he only lasted three years. You just never know.

#4. RICK IS ONE OF KIND

I will use Rick O'Connell's name because you all know him and care for him a great deal. He was a master in his relations with people. I have never seen a relationship like he had with the many Boards of Education he served. He didn't dominate them, nor did he ever intimidate them, but he was always in control of the situation. Rick was only the second superintendent this district ever had, being here for over twenty-two years. But Rick's greatest strength was hiring outstanding people and then letting them do their job.

When you have a team of Mrs. Ellen Bartlett, Dr. Pat Grippe, and Bill Reimer, you are Super Bowl bound, and Rick was the coach.

#5. THE NEW KID ON THE BLOCK..DR. JIM

When Rick O'Connell retired, many people had mixed emotions about his leaving. I was grateful for the many years of service he gave to this district, but I knew that the district would survive. And besides, there were a lot of fish out there that had to be caught.

I also asked myself, why would anyone want this job, in spite of the fact the superintendent was inheriting the best district in the state? After a very intensive national search for the new superintendent, the Board of Education found him just up the road along I-25. Dr. Jim Christensen would become the new boss, and he has proven to be a great catch.

He hasn't been here long enough to pass Dr. Davis's test, but I am sure he will be here for many years to come. He may cost a little more each year (they all do), but he will be worth it.

The "Dream Team"
of Rick,
Bill and Ellen ...
Superbowl Bound

**Cutting the ribbon to officially open
Soaring Hawk Elementary School:
Superintendent Jim Christensen
and Principal Jill Donley**

SENIOR CITIZENS PLAY BIG ROLE IN DOUGLAS COUNTY

Many of you old timers will remember those signs that read. "WE WANT YOU," as Uncle Sam pointed his finger at you. Of course, he wanted men and women to serve in the armed forces during World War II. While Uncle Sam may have wanted you, the Douglas County School district wants senior citizens over 60 to come and work in our schools. The district has budgeted for 90 men and women to do so, and they can work up to 125 hours and earn $6.50 an hour.

This program began in 1989, when the money could be used for partial payment of taxes. This was then called the Senior Tax Exchange. Times have changed as have laws, and today the program is called the Senior Volunteer Program. Money can now be used for anything. I was one of the first seniors to work in this program. I served as a tutor in the Title One program at Acres Green Elementary.

I believe that one of the strengths of this program is that the district encourages and allows the volunteers to use their strengths and desires. Some enjoy working in the library while others would rather work directly with children. I have been fortunate to be allowed to go into the classrooms and be "JUST A TEACHER". I work with children from grades two through five in teaching Douglas County History and Geography skills.

Each year, at the end of the year, there is a wonderful banquet served for the volunteers and their principals. It is always held in various restaurants around the county. The coordinator of the program, Mrs. Debbie Novotny, always has a very elegant and interesting program, to show how much the district cares about these men and women.

One of the faults of our society is the lack of contact young people have with their elders. Many children are separated from their grandparents and are not able to have that interaction with them. Consequently, children have no idea of what life was like in those earlier days.

In the classes that I teach in Colorado and Douglas County History, the children can't wait to hear another story from the past. They can't believe that the first TV I bought in 1949 was a nine-inch, black and white set that I paid $1200.00 for.

They are shocked to learn that I did baby-sitting for 25 cents an evening, not an hour. But perhaps the thing they enjoy the most are slides I have taken over the many years. They love the animals from Africa and old farm machinery from our countryside.

As the program has developed over the years, so too has the number of men who are now volunteering. I think it is the wonderful devil-eggs that brings them back each year. They are a profound attraction for me.

If you would like to come to your neighborhood school and "do your thing", just contact Debbie at 303-387-0100.

As the old Uncle Sam sign said, "WE WANT YOU." and let me add, " We NEED you."

"Sometimes the hardest time in Senior Volunteering is getting up and down in those little chairs."

NATIONAL TEACHING ACADEMY...
AN IDEA LONG OVERDUE

By the beginning of the 20 century, ladies and gentlemen were attending colleges to earn a teaching license to teach in a community. Prior to that, the teacher in town was the lady (single) who was the best reader and willing to work for chicken-feed. Many were granted provisional certificates while they began to attend classes in local teacher's colleges.

To keep up with the increasing demand for teachers, many states established teachers colleges. These were schools where teachers could take courses that would help them in the classroom. The requirements from state to state were not the same. Most of the professors had never taught in a classroom and knew little more than their students. The biggest advantage these educational neophytes had was they were single, willing to work for very little and very dedicated to the children.

Although the National Education Association was founded in 1857, it really did very little to aid the professions. Its leaders were administrators, and never tried to do a whole lot for teachers. Its purpose was to improve the quality of life and improve teaching conditions. Let me tell you how they helped me. When I was hired to teach sixth grade in Rock Island, my salary was $3200.00 a year, no medical benefits, and my class consisted of 34 eager children. On my first day, the principal came to me and asked for $5.00 for NEA dues. When I told her I could not afford that much , she became very indignant and said she would pay my dues so the school could have 100 percent.

As time went on, many colleges began to offer education courses so teachers could be certified. When I returned to St. Ambrose College, after a seven year layoff, it had become a university and now offered courses in education. The law was that a person had to have taken 24 hours of education courses to get a certificate. At this school, one person taught all of the education courses. While he was a very nice priest, he never taught me anything I ever used in a classroom. We got along very well, and I received an "A" in all of his courses. I am sure that many teachers from that generation could tell similar stories.

While we have the Air Force Academy at Colorado Springs, Annapolis Naval Academy in Maryland, West Point in New York, and the Coast Guard Academy in New London CT, to prepare the defenders of our country, why not organize Academies for the teachers of our country?

ACADEMIES AND LOCATION
I am submitting my ideas for this plan. How would you change it?

LOCATION OF ACADEMIES
1. Locate academies in five different locations in small colleges. Possible locations hypothetical.
    A. Idaho State to serve North-western states
    B. Arkansas State to serve lower Midwest
    C. Indiana State to serve upper Mid-west
    D. Connecticut State serves North- eastern area
    E. South Carolina State to serve South- east

STAFFING
1. Applications for the director of each academy
2. Hiring of directors done by screening committee at each school
3. Teachers will be employed from local school districts in each area. Salary to be paid by local district. Teachers will work for two years at academy

REQUIREMENTS OF STUDENTS FOR ACCEPTANCE
1. Graduate in top 20 per cent of class.
2. GPA of at least 2.7
3. Recommendations from 3 high school staff
4. Recommendations from employers or non-teaching person (minister, counselor, etc.)

CURRICULUM AND GRADUATION REQUIREMENTS

CURRICULUM
1ST YEAR. This year will be spent in selection of a major outside of Education. Complete half of major in year one. Begin to keep journal for information you will use in your final thesis for graduation.

2ND YEAR. Complete major requirements (16 HOURS) Courses In education problems and strategies. Spend one day each week in observation in local schools.

3RD YEAR Spend three days each week in observation and practice teaching. Must observe classes at all economic levels in local schools.

4th YEAR Teach 4 days a week in local schools for first semester. Student will be paid for this teaching. Work one day each week with seminars, personal tutoring and/or other teaching activities.

Second semester will be spent in teaching full time in a local school.   Will be assigned a mentor to work with from local school. Student will be paid full rate of local district. Attend two evening seminars with fellow teachers.

GRADUATION REQUIREMENTS
1. 16 HOURS IN MAJOR FIELD
    (Math, Science, Reading)
2. 6 HOURS IN EDUCATIONAL
    PROBLEMS/ STRATEGIES
3. 10 HOURS OF CLASSROOM OBSERVATION
    IN 3rd YEAR
4. 16 HOURS IN FULL TIME TEACHING
    (4th YEAR)
5. SUBMIT THESIS, USING INFORMATION FROM
    YOUR DAILY JOURNAL

Students will graduate with a Bachelor's Degree, Advanced BSA in Education.

All students who graduate will be employed by a district at a 20 percent higher than regular local salary schedule.

The purpose of this plan is to educate teachers with a major in one academic field. It is also intended to reduce those Ed. 101 methods classes.

THE DRAFT IS NEEDED FOR EVERYONE

During this Iraq War, there has been a lot of debate about bringing back the draft. We all know that there were not enough soldiers in the all enlisted armed forces to fight this war. So the Army Reserves were brought in to make up the shortage. Add to that the terrific work these men and women did during the hurricane season this year.

When I graduated from High School, I immediately enlisted in the Unites States Navy. I was assigned to serve in the Hospital Corps as a Corpsman. I was sent to Great Lakes Naval Station in Waukegan, Illinois for basic training. From there I was shipped to Bainbridge, MD for six weeks of medical training. Since the war was winding down, I was then returned to Great Lakes to care for the thousands of wounded sailors and marines.

I have found that most men and women who served in World War II feel good about that period of their lives. Many in the Viet Nam conflict would probably not agree. But most veterans I talk to feel that their time in the military was good for them in many ways.

For many years, I have advocated the reinstatement of the draft for all men and women ages 18 to 21. I feel that this age group could benefit from the discipline of the military and increase their patriotism by serving their country.

I don't mean a military draft, but rather a service to country organization. Some in this draft would serve to defend our country. But there are so many other needs we have that could be met with the help of a citizen service corps.

We learned from the hurricanes how unprepared this country was for an emergency of that magnitude. There were just not people in place to react to this tragic incident. We have learned here in Colorado how badly people were needed when we had the Hayman Fire.

We all hope that a Sept 11 will never happen again. But inside we know it will, and it has been proven that we are not ready to deal with catastrophes.

The young people in my program would be involved in many ways. They can be trained in medial assistance; they can pursue a career in electronics. They can receive their college future as so many did with the G.I. Bill, when millions of us were afforded the opportunity to go to college and get paid for it.

I have lived through many wars, and served in one. But the only time I felt like I was a part of supporting my country was during World War II. During Viet Nam and now Iraq, nothing has been asked of me. Certainly, nothing has been asked of those 18-20 year olds in this conflict.

We saw how Americans can respond to an event like the hurricanes. Money poured in from everywhere. Food, clothing, and other supplies came in from all over the country. But that is not proactive. We should not have to wait for hundreds to die before we assume the responsibility to our country.

I have often wished that I would have made the U.S. Navy my career. When you are in the military, every day is a challenge to make your country a better place.

My idea of a service corps will never come to pass. This generation is too selfish and self centered to ever develop that feeling of patriotism, but I still think it is a good idea.

This was the beginning of something that made a big difference in my life. I was forced to go from boyhood to manhood in six weeks.

THE PROOF IS IN THE PUDDING,
YOU CAN MAKE A DIFFERENCE

Throughout this book you have read about how I have made a difference in the lives of many and how individuals have made a big difference in my life. As a teacher, you have a unique opportunity to make a big difference in the lives of those people you touch. Many of you will learn that many will turn out to be life long friendships.

Last year I had something happen that I believe was the highlight of my 48 years in teaching, and I want to share that with you.

42 years ago, a young seventh grade girl, Patsy Bell, stopped by my classroom one day after school. She had with her a large door screen. On it she had made a picture of a Madonna and Child, using needlepoint with a window screen backing on a wooden frame. I was so impressed that I began to make similar pictures. Over the years, I have done several schools and houses.

When I moved to Colorado, I became very interested in the history of Douglas County. Thanks to the wonderful book, *Fading Past ,the Story of Douglas County* by Susan Appleby, I learned enough about our county to begin to teach it to fourth graders in three of our schools.

I also at that time began to make yarn pictures of historic places in this county. When the new Philip Miller Library opened in Castle Rock in 2003, I donated 24 of these yarn pictures to the historic section of this facility. The remainder of the pictures I use to introduce the unit that I teach.

As I was making these pictures, I began to think that I bet Patsy would like to know what I was doing with what she taught me. But how do you locate a girl that was in your class 42 years ago, especially a girl who probably has a married name?

After contacting several sources for a year, I finally located her in a small town in Maine. I contacted her by e-mail, and we began a long friendship that continues through today.

A few months later, she called and said that her class was having its high school reunion, and that several of my former students would be there. She said if I was in the area to come to the reunion dinner. It so happened that I was on my way to visit my cousin in Wisconsin, and I had to go right through Rock Island.

That evening at the hotel there were 14 of my former students in attendance. It was so wonderful to see them all again. During the intermission, one of my former students went to the microphone and introduced me and the other man teacher who taught fifth grade in our building. Then he asked me to come to the microphone, and I could not believe what came next.

These former students had put together a notebook, filled with pictures of their families now and personal letters to me, recalling all of the projects we had done back in sixth grade. I am enclosing some samples of those letters in this book. What pleased me most was that nine of these women had become teachers because of their experiences with me.

Am I being facetious for showing you these things? Probably so, but I just want you to know that these things can happen to you because you are "JUST A TEACHER." Never let an opportunity pass you by to make a difference in someone's life.

Over the years, I have made more than 100 pictures of historic places in Douglas County. I donated several to the new library, and many others I use in the classroom. Here are just a few.

This is a picture of those students who attended their class reunion in Rock Island, Illinois on July 19, 2003. These people were all students in my sixth grade class at Eugene Field Elementary School in 1956.

I am also inserting some of the letters I received from several of these people. Yes, one person CAN make a difference, and that person can be you.

July 19, 2003

Dear Mr. O'Hern,

So glad to have this opportunity to say "Thank You!" for the wonderful foundation for learning you set in my life during Sixth Grade (1961-62) at Eugene Field School.

You taught about diagraming sentences, developing debate arguments, writing research papers, taking spelling tests in ink, and competing in "College Bowl"-like contests. You always challenged us to work to the "best of our ability—and then some! I remember when you were asked why you pushed us so hard. You replied, "Preparation for life." You prepared us well. Thank you!

It's interesting how we remember some of the "little" things that have helped us over the years. Whenever I meet a Canadian, I recall your tip on remembering the provinces, "You be a sharp man on questions" — for Yukon, British Columbia, Alberta, etc. In my job as a speech language pathologist I'm often reminded of the parts of speech and grammar tips you gave us ("Adjectives — what kind? how many?" etc.)

Most of all, I remember you being a fine human being (with a great smile and sense of humor) who really cared about us. You made learning exciting and worth the effort.

Thanks for the memories!

Warmly,
Sherill (David) Condry
103 Mtn. View Ct.
Medford, OR 97501

("Bunny")

Memories of Mr. O'Hern

I've shared quite a few memories of sixth grade with you over the past few months, but I wanted to reiterate that your call in September was one of the nicest surprises of my life. I have always considered you the best teacher I ever had.

Thinking back on what you had us doing, I wonder if you ever slept at night! The library projects, debating at Augustana, state research project, demonstration speech, essay writing, and college bowl were amazing learning projects. And...

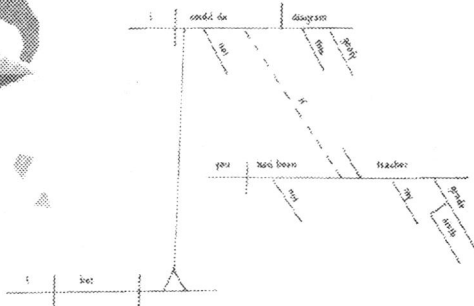

Thank you for your contribution to my education and for your renewed friendship.

Patsy

Patsy Bell Meisner

To Mr. Orlow

We were the lucky ones, the kids born just after WWII.
We were the Baby Boomers and had the best of everything,
including you, as our teacher.

And now it is time to say
THANK YOU

For pushing us to reach up to achieve
For leading us in the classroom
For giving us solid values that have carried us through our lives
For your dedication to our education
For being the model that set the standard for all other teachers
For the inspiration to those of us that teach now
For being the dynamic figure the classroom that makes students
remember you with respect and joy after 40 years have passed.

We were the lucky ones, you were the teacher that stood at the entrance to
our futures and gave us the instructions to begin it.

With Love & Thanks
Barbara "Cookie" Fracassi — STEVE

July 19, 2003

163

Sixth Grade
Top of the Grad School Food Chain!

"First learn your teacher, then learn your subject."

The Library Project.
Canada Today.
"A Theme a Week" – I just found mine.
Mercury astronauts.
Career Reports.
Good music while we studied – I still like good music
while I'm working.
Book reports – my mom shared her good books.
Diagramming sentences – I always loved the logic
and the sense of order. I still do it in my head!
Speeches – Horrors!
"Regurgitating" what we know.
Time Line for South American history – the joy of eating coffee beans!
College Bowl – forgetting what ICBM means – argh!
Listening to the "Poe-ettes" as a fifth grader. Copied (shamelessly)
Craig Shoemaker's delivery of "Seein' Things" as a sophomore at Rocky
in '65 and again in college in '91. Aced them both.
Grammar is still my friend.
Coming back to school following an injury. You knew the meaning of the
work coccyx – horrors again!
All primed for "Mr. Jennings" in 7th grade – disappointed to get Mr.
Isaacs. He turned out to be a good teacher, a neighbor to my folks and
a dear to them friend for life.
Failing my first essay test – getting an A+ on the corresponding
objective test – you felt my pain & my joy –
helped me learn how to cope.
Getting organized.
Kennedy.
Stories about your grandmother.

Great expectations for us.
High confidence in us.
Letting us know how much you really did like us
and how much you loved teaching sixth grade.

Motor   Thanks for so much!
          Jane Sedrel Noble

164

MY MOTHER.. A WOMAN WHO RANKS
AMONG THE BEST

On June 13, 2001, ALMA O'HERN, my Mother, passed away at the age of 92. She had undergone a hip transplant. When they returned her to the nursing home, they placed her in a wheel chair. When I saw her, she said to me, "Jim, I will not live this way. I am going to die."

I jokingly said to her, " Well don't do it on the 13th. I have a party for the kids planned."

When I left her, she told the nurses to cut off all food and medications. She then went to bed and remained there for five days. On the 13th, the home called me and said that Alma had just died. I heard this as I was leaving for the party.

Each day, the *Rocky Mountain News* publishes an obituary page. Many well known people have their picture included with the item about them. My Mother was not included on the obituary page as she was only famous to her family and friends. But there are some things about her that could qualify her for that page, and you need to know them.

Although she never created any economic policies, nor did she ever advise any of the Presidents, she had the ability to balance all of her budgets. I can remember growing up that at the end of the month, Mother had a budget surplus of 25 cents. Our family would then vote on whether we wanted to go to the movie or buy a pint of ice cream. But we couldn't do both.

Alma never won the Cy Young Award for pitching like Bob Gibson or Nolen Ryan ever did, but she was considered by most of the 10 year olds that lived in our neighborhood as the "Best Softball Pitcher" on the block.

She was never in Peggy Lee's class, but she could sing every popular song during the age of the big bands. She and I listened to the radio each evening to the broadcast of the big bands from WGN Chicago. They broadcast from the Aragon and Trianon ballrooms in the Windy City.

Mother was never the head chef at any of the famous restaurants, but she could dish up a plate of golden fried chicken like you never tasted before. Along with it would be a platter of fried noodles (sorry no secret recipe to give you).

This year, we lost such famous entertainers as Johnny Carson and Eddie Albert. While Mother was never an entertainer like these men, she could make those tears turn to smiles at the drop of the hat.

We also lost this year such lawyers as Johnny Cochran and Justice Rehnquist. But even they could not match the record in law that Mother had. She never lost an argument to my Dad, and I never won an argument with her.

Estee Lauder passed away last year. He left an empire of cosmetics. Mother could have been the best salesperson for those products. She was the head cosmetician at Walgreens for 40 years.

Finally, while Mother never won a Pulitzer Prize for writing, her letters to me while I was in the Navy would match the writing of even Hemingway.

I leave you with this story. Until her last year, Mother had her own apartment in Castle Rock. She loved to just sit and look at the mountains from her living room window. But she could never get it straight as to which were the hills and which were the mountains.

Her wish was to be cremated, and we took her ashes to the foothills and scattered them. As we did, we told her.

" Now Mother, you have a long time to figure out which are the hills and which are the mountains."

I know she smiled at that one.

Dr. OHen is the Best

WHO IS DR. JAMES O'HERN

James was born James Herbert Munro on July 24, 1928 in Moline Illinois. He attended schools in Rock Island, Illinois and Burlington, Iowa. He enlisted in the United States Navy as a medical corpsman in 1946. However, before he left for duty, his stepfather of 15 years legally adopted him and gave him the name "O'Hern."

He returned to attend St. Ambrose College in 1948, but he left school in 1951 to work as a Management Trainee at Sears Roebuck. After five years with Sears, he returned to St. Ambrose and earned his Bachelors Degree in Secondary Education.

He began his teaching career as a sixth grade teacher in Rock Island at Eugene Field Elementary School. After four years, he earned his Master's Degree in Elementary Education, and he became a principal for six years in Rock Island.

In 1968, James moved to Galesburg, Illinois and became the principal of Steele Middle School. He took early retirement in 1985, and became the editor of a historical magazine. He then served two years on the Galesburg Board of Education.

Since coming to Colorado in 1987, Jim has been extremely active in the Douglas County School District. Most of his experiences here have been described in this book.

Jim is now 77 plus and spends every day in a classroom at either Sand Creek Elementary or Eagle Ridge Elementary. He plays the trumpet in the Castle Rock Town band and does needlepoint pictures of historic places in Douglas County. To date, he has completed and placed in every high school and middle school a picture of that school. He is now working on completing all of the elementary schools.

He has touched the lives of many children and adults in his life, and he hopes that from reading his writings, you too will find ways to make a difference in the lives of the people that you touch.

Just A Teacher

HOW ONE PERSON <u>CAN</u> MAKE A DIFFERENCE

by **Dr. James O'Hern**

$14.99
+ $2.00 Shipping/handling

I.S.B.N. 1-59879-082-X

Order Online at:
www.authorstobelievein.com
or contact
jjohern@msn.com

By Phone Toll Free at:
1-877-843-1007